Jesus Heals The Brokenhearted

(Overcoming Heartache with
Biblical Principles)

BY HOA TONG

This book is dedicated to Jesus Christ my Lord who brought me out of the prison of pain, Leslie, my wife, and Zoe, Lukas and Judah, our children who have been my inspiration and motivation to make a difference in the world.

It is also dedicated to my family who survived a war in Vietnam and crossed an ocean. My parents, Hai and Khanh, my siblings, Qui, Micke, and Minnie, my aunt, Cecile, and my grandmother Le Chi Tran.

This book is also in memory of my brethren who are in the arms of my Savior – Pastor Max & Elizabeth Briones, Elder Leon Cotillon, Brother Raymond, Hanh Do, Amber Bazan, Eric Dominno, Charmaine Angus, Mike Jones, and Dawn Basilio, who all taught me so much about inner healing.

Special thanks to Lisa Mendricks for all the editing help and the Members and Ministers of Freedom for praying for, supporting, and believing in me all these years.

Foreword

The book *"Jesus Heals the Brokenhearted"* sincerely goes into a reality of what it takes to heal a broken heart. Dr. Hoa Tong is a powerful ambassador of this message. He is one of the only men in the world I'd call a true ambassador of love.

This book is his message and he has helped heal many people through what is written in this phenomenal book.

If you are looking for a new beginning, "Jesus Heals the Brokenhearted" is the place to start.

Clyde Rivers, Ph.D.
Ambassador at Large
Republic of Burundi, Africa

Representative To The United Nations
Interfaith Peace-Building Initiative

Co-Chairman,
Congressional Prayer Conference of Washington D.C.

Endorsements

God's people are blessed to pick up this amazing life giving book from my friend, Dr. Hoa Tong. Every time true revelation is birthed in the earth through a servant of God like Dr. Tong, it's a sign of God's intent to express his powerful love to heal the brokenhearted for millions of hurting people worldwide. Everyone who reads this truth will be healed, from leaders to all the saints in the body of Christ. Let the heart-healing revolution begin.

Dr. Mike Kingsley
President/Founder, Latter Glory World Mission

Pastor Hoa Tong, has written a blueprint for anyone wanting wholeness and healing from relational pain. "Jesus Heals the Brokenhearted" is for anyone wanting to move forward and find genuine breakthrough and life change. I recommend you get a copy today.

Troy Marshall
President/Founder
Troy Marshall Ministries
Lionsgate Leadership & Missions Institute

"Jesus Heals the Brokenhearted" is a book that speaks about two levels of truth. Truth is like a shovel that can cover or uncover every broken area of your life, dreams and destiny. One shovel of truth says that you have been hurt, wounded and left for dead. This shovel is ready to dig your grave. The other shovel says that there is a way to dig your way to total healing. Dr. Hoa Tong experienced a painful situation in his own life, but the Lord interceded with biblical principles which gave way to the shovel of truth being placed in his hands. I have had the

personal pleasure of seeing Dr. Tong pass this same shovel to so many who were already knee-deep in the burial process with the wrong truth of their situation. This is "the book" for those who are suffering with heart conditions that seem terminal. Reach out and grab the shovel of truth contained in this book that buries your past and heals your future.

Pastor Donna Smiley-Young
Director/Founder , Fields of Glory International

My great friend Dr. Hoa Tong was prompted by the Holy Spirit to write this encouraging life-changing book "Jesus Heals the Broken Hearted." II Corinthians 1:3-4 says He is the God of all comfort! And, "to comfort others as you yourself are comforted." The Holy Spirit, the Comforter, was sent to comfort those who are broken and crushed in spirit. I pray as you read this book that you will experience His presence and receive His comfort and peace. This is an amazing book and truly inspired by the Holy Spirit. Thank you, Dr. Hoa for being obedient to write the book and for the awesome revelations you have received straight from the throne room of God.

Dr. Sonny Lara
Senior Pastor Star of David Ministries
Golden Rule Goodwill Ambassador
Director/Founder, Firehouse Community Development Corporation

Hoa Tong has written a masterpiece that opens the inner chamber & deepest part of the human soul. As a subject matter expert in the field of human performance I recommend this book to anyone who needs the healing of a broken heart. It personally ministered to me and helped my heart heal and love even greater!

Ron Kardashian NSCA, CPT
Chief Executive Advisor | Strategist | Coach

True understanding of being healed from painful brokenness can only come from those who have truly experienced such pain. Dr. Hoa Tong, the author of this book, "Jesus Heals the Brokenhearted" uses the truth of God's Word to share how those with such experiences can be made whole and healed through the loving hands and power of Jesus. He clearly uses the scriptures as proof that God is close to the brokenhearted and desires to heal all those who are broken, wounded and hurting. Dr. Hoa Tong is truly a man of God who demonstrates the love and passion for the lost and hurting in his everyday walk with Christ.

Dr. Linda A. Lara
Founder/Director of (SEAPLL)
School of Apostolic/Prophetic Lions & Lioness
Golden Rule Goodwill Ambassador
Co-Senior Pastor
Star of David Ministries

Pastor Hoa expresses the heart of God in the pages of this book. He shares personal life experiences with sound Biblical truths that give us a glimpse into the heart of God. Pastor Hoa is a voice that God is raising up for this generation. This book is a recommended read.

J.R. Gonzalez
Apostle, Founding Pastor
Dominion Life Center Church

"Wow", what great insight and transparency by my dear friend, Dr. Hoa Tong. While I was reading, I experienced inner healing from my own past and I believe the same will transpire for all who read it as well. Dr. Hoa brings out the essential heart and compassion of Jesus that is crucial for all those who engage in the affairs of life. Through his life and experiences, Dr. Hoa brings out the insights of

the Lord for our benefit. I thank the Lord for Dr. Hoa, a gift to the entire body of Christ and for being a fellow soldier in this last days army. I highly recommend this book to be read by all believers in their walk with Jesus Christ for personal and ministerial revelation. (Luke 4:18), (2 Corinthians 5:16-21)

*Abraham Abu-Hamid
Founder, Senior Minister
Katallassō Word Ministries Inc.*

Pastor Hoa Tong has written a book that is a roadmap back to wholeness. Every chapter of this book has principles that are scriptural, powerful, and applicable. From his own brokenness and healing he has drawn wisdom that has been tested by fire. If you know someone with a broken heart get this book into their hands. I strongly believe this book will help many souls.

*Quoc Nguyen
Young Adult & Youth Pastor
River of Life Church*

In "Jesus Heals the Brokenhearted", Dr. Hoa Tong reveals an intensely personal encounter with heartbreak and the pain, confusion, and despair that often accompanies it. His unique story, scripture, and biblical perspective is cleverly interwoven throughout the book in a way that helps reveal God's road to hope and healing. In a world where heartbreak is a commonplace, "Jesus Heals the Brokenhearted" is a must-read.

*Jeff Dumo
Partner, CEO
Array Interactive / Experiential Digital Agency*

Dr Hoa bears all in his book "Jesus Heals the Brokenhearted"!
Daring to share his personal experiences while imparting powerful
tools for deliverance and healing. In particular I found the prayers he
offers at the end of each chapter to be a powerful source of activation
and Healing for the Spirit, Soul and Body. I'm sure you will enjoy this
reader-friendly book as I have. Thank you Dr. Hoa for writing this
book, my friend and brother in arms,

Tony Menjivar
Apostle, Senior Pastor
Love International Outreach, San Francisco

All solutions have value if there is strong proof presented by
eyewitnesses and a life witness. It's because of this principle that I
present my own life instead of my words as a powerful testimony to
the healing love of Jesus flowing through Dr. Hoa Tong's Ministry. It
has changed my life. From a broken marriage and living in the lowest
depths of society to becoming a pastor over the care of the Lord's
ministry. How can I write the words for this type of beautiful miracle?

Israel Nguyen
Senior Pastor
Grace Community Vietnamese Church

"Jesus Heals the Brokenhearted" demonstrates the message of grace
and shows amazing insight of how God desires to heal His people.
Whatever type of heartache you've suffered, this book reveals that no
matter what comes, God is faithful. I believe there is a truth expressed
when Dr. Hoa wrote, "I revisited my altar in the wilderness of
heartache and again, He came." This powerful insight reminds us that
God is and always will be faithful, and no matter the circumstance, He
will continually deliver you. This word so ministered to me because it
revealed God's compassion. He will meet you again and again to keep

you free. This book, "Jesus Heals the Brokenhearted", is a word for every believer, and a must-read.

Robert Sanchez
Prophet
Prophetic First Fruits International Ministries

The most undeniably pure ministry of Jesus to be mantled is to heal the brokenhearted. I've known Pastor Hoa Tong to be anointed in this ministry. Pastor Hoa is the real deal.

Reverend Neva Lema
Senior Pastor
Restoration City Church

In this book, "Jesus Heals the Brokenhearted", Pastor Hoa has hit the bullseye by laying down his experience and practical principles on how we can appropriate this healing in every area of our lives that have been made available in Jesus Christ. I recommend this easy-to-read book that packs a lot of power in each chapter.

Reverend Ronaldo Banatao
Senior Pastor
Lion's Heart Christian Ministries (Corazon de Leon)
Madrid, Spain

Table of Contents

Foreword..iii

Endorsements..v

Introduction...xiii

CHAPTER 1: Journey to the Center of the Heart............................1

CHAPTER 2: The Wounded Healer 5

CHAPTER 3: Realize God is Near and Run to Him 11

CHAPTER 4: See the Big Picture. God is Still in Control..............19

CHAPTER 5: Get Better. Not Bitter...27

CHAPTER 6: Come Against the Force of Shame 35

CHAPTER 7: Reach for Tomorrow..41

CHAPTER 8: Find Somebody to Love 47

CHAPTER 9: A Friend in Need is a Friend Indeed........................57

CHAPTER 10: Pursue an Attitude of Gratitude 65

CHAPTER 11: One Day at a Time 71

CHAPTER 12: Believe for a Happy Ending 77

About the Author, Hoa Tong...83

About Freedom Worship Center 87

Introduction

It never occurred to me to write about my personal experience of emotional healing until I was repeatedly told that my testimonies would help many people. I am forever grateful for what Jesus Christ has done for me. The good news I seek to spread is that He longs to do the same for the multitudes He loves. Whosoever will, let them come. Truly, He is not a respecter of persons.

The circumstances that led to my broken heart are not unique. Millions, if not untold billions of people all over the world and throughout history, have experienced heartache. However, it is my belief that very few have been able to overcome it and lead happy productive lives afterwards. We see evidence of this in love songs around the world. There will always be songs about a broken heart because none of us are immune to hurt or failure in our relationships or the tragic things that happen to us. It is a part of life, just as birth and death is.

Some would argue that we will never have sorrow when we receive Christ. How untrue is that statement. Troubles will come in this life. Jesus said so in John 16:33, but thank God that He has overcome the world.

My hope is to effectively reveal to you who God and His Son, Jesus Christ, truly is through the Scriptures–the Healer of broken hearts. He is the same yesterday, today and forever. Take courage, feeble heart, though sorrow may endure for the night, joy comes in the morning.

"Heavenly Father in Jesus' name, I pray for the person reading this book. I ask that You would by Your power and love, heal their broken heart. Make them whole again that they may bring Your

healing touch to others. Grant them the strength to endure their time of suffering until the new day dawns in their hearts and they may rejoice again with renewed strength, vision and purpose. Reveal to them the Christ in all His glory so that the gates of hell shall not prevail in their lives any longer. Be healed in Jesus' mighty name! Amen."

CHAPTER 1

Journey to the Center of the Heart

"The heart will break, yet brokenly live on."

– Byron

The Day the Earth Stood Still

That day in October of 1994 began like any other – a quick call was made to my long-time girlfriend to plan how we would spend the day together. We had a small disagreement, but that was not out of the ordinary. We had been dating for over six years since our late teens and had talked numerous times about marriage. We were both committed believers in Christ and kept our relationship upright before God. Things were almost too good to be true.

I've always had a childhood fear of marriage. My parents were divorced when I was eleven years old. It wasn't until I received Christ at the age of eighteen that He began to quench my personal fears of failing at marriage in the future. On that October day, I was motivated to purchase an engagement ring. I was excited and anxious to propose to her that night. She knew nothing of my plans and gladly went with me to one of our favorite places. Atop a hill overlooking the sunset of a beautiful California evening, I asked her to marry me and showed her the diamond ring. It was the day that I had hoped for, prayed for, and believed would happen. Tears began to flow down her cheeks as she gladly said, "Yes." I really thought we were a match made in heaven. I was called to preach and she was gifted to sing. The following months, however, would only reveal the truth.

Four months into our engagement, signs of trouble began to surface. Her attendance and commitment in our local Church began to wane and our communication began to decrease gradually. I hoped to brighten our spirits with a romantic dinner on Valentine's Day. Dinner went well and afterwards we arrived at her parent's house to spend time together. As I held her in my arms and pondered our future together, a strong premonition came into my being. It seemed as if a voice deep inside of me was predicting that I would not be with her much longer and that her heart toward me was changing. I quickly dismissed it as my own personal insecurities and held her to comfort myself from the fear that was now growing within me. As we said goodnight and I sat in my car, the premonition came again only stronger. This time, I knew it was the Lord. The revelation of my future hit with such impact and force that I could not hold back the tears that streamed down my face.

Like Mary who hid the "sayings in her heart" regarding her son as the Messiah, I, too, awaited to see whether this prophecy would come to pass. Three months later, after the Word of the Lord had come to me, practically all communication lines were cut between us. Unreturned calls came with regularity. Excuses mounted as to why she could not come to the phone or answer the door. I knew in my heart that God was merciful by warning me months in advance to prepare me for the fall out.

Seasons change and our long-term relationship was set to end that fateful summer morning in 1995. The night before, I had made a decision to catch her before she went to work. She would have no excuses now seeing me face to face. I knew it had to happen and yet I dreaded it with all my being. I knocked on her door nervously. Her father answered and called her, as if knowing why I had come. Slowly, she appeared in the hallway and approached me silently. "I knew you were coming today." She said. We sat down on the same sofas that we had held each other on for the last seven years, but this time, searching for words to somehow bridge the great gap between us was difficult.

As she handed me back the engagement ring, I asked her all the "why's" in my heart. Why end it? Why say "yes" in the first place? Why stay with me all these years? Why can't we just pray together for an answer like we had done so many times in the past? Why? Why? Why? To all my inquiries, I got no answers. "I don't know and I can't tell you why." were her responses. Anger arose in me and I felt robbed of all the years of my youth. I knew that if it ended that day, I would not come back. The pain was almost unbearable. Unbelief, shame, fear, and sorrow pierced me like arrows in that decisive moment. I felt like a failure. I felt like I had missed God. I felt like I had let everyone down - my parents, her parents, mutual friends, our Church family, my co-workers who congratulated us, and my now ex- fiancée. But most of all, I felt lost and so terribly alone. I had just lost a part of my heart and soul in that hour. I left her house for the final time and whispered a heartfelt cry to God Almighty, "Help me, Father."

CHAPTER 2

The Wounded Healer

" You never know Jesus is all you need until Jesus is all you have."
– Corrie Ten Boom

I t hurt. It hurt a lot. Leaving her house that day was the hardest thing I ever had to do at that point in my life. I knew I was walking away from a marriage, a family, and a future that I had envisioned for myself. Entering my car, my first thought was to find God. I had to find Him no matter what the cost. I knew from His Word that He was the only One who could heal me. I was in ministry at the time as a new Assistant Pastor of a small church in San Jose, California. I arrived at the Church and entered its sacred sanctuary." *It's just you and me Jesus"*, I thought to myself as I prostrated myself before Him and let all the pain in my being pour out. I cried and cried. I wept until I thought there was not a tear left in my body, and then I wept again.

The Anointed One

"The Spirit of the Lord is upon Me, because He hath anointed Me to preach the gospel to the poor. He has sent me to heal the broken hearted, to proclaim deliverance to the captives and recovering of sight to the blind, to set at liberty them that are bruised" -Luke 4:18

Jesus is called the Christ. The word Christ means the Anointed One. When Jesus began His earthly ministry, He read from the Prophet Isaiah and declared that the Spirit of the Lord had *anointed* Him or chosen and empowered Him to do certain things. One of the things He is anointed or empowered to do is *heal the broken hearted*. It's what He does best. It's one of the reasons why He came to Earth.

God has empowered Jesus Christ to be our Healer. There is no hurt or pain that God cannot comfort through His Son. In fact, Jesus was bruised so that we could be made whole. He was the sacrifice for our sins, sorrows, and pain. He has suffered the pains of humanity, all of it, making Him a great Savior.

"How do you know God knows what I feel", you ask?

Let's take a closer look at His dealings with mankind throughout Biblical history and see why men call Him the Wounded Healer.

Adam And Eve

We all know the creation story. It is the tale of a God who lovingly created His masterpiece- Adam or man. He gave him the perfect mate in the woman, Eve. He gave him the perfect home in Eden and the perfect job as the ruler over the whole world. It is also the greatest story of love and loss ever. The God who breathed life into a lump of clay to make him a living soul is also the same God who experienced betrayal by him. Imagine the pain God felt when they willingly disobeyed Him to serve another master–satan. Their Divine relationship was severed and the trust between them shattered.

This merciful God sought to make amends and recapture the lost intimacy they shared. Adam and Eve's children, however, would also spurn His love over the ages and even deny His existence to this present day.

The Israelites

We also know that many centuries later, He called a people to Himself through His covenant with the man, Abraham. This would be His very own people- a nation that would know His statutes, laws and ways. A nation solely set apart to know Him and walk with Him. A people after His own heart, expected to be devoted to Him and no other. Yet they too had their affairs with other gods made with men's hands. Their stormy relationship over the centuries was marked by periods of faithfulness and unfaithfulness, reconciliation and then separation, peace and war. Imagine the pain He felt when He decided to send a representative, His own Son, into their world only to be scorned and rejected, hated and hounded, and eventually tortured and killed.

The Twelve Disciples

We know that while on earth, His only begotten Son called to Himself twelve men out of all the men in the world to be His followers or personal assistants whom He would train on a daily basis. We know that one of them was to betray Him in the end. As it turned out, all twelve abandoned Him and Peter, the one whom He entrusted the keys of His kingdom to would publicly deny Him not once, but three times in anger.

Now take a mental picture of His trial before the people of Jerusalem. The Roman Governor, Pontius Pilate was willing to release Him or another prisoner based on the choice of the people. These were the same people that He healed, held, and taught and whom He fed, blessed and raised back to life. These same people now cried for the release of another prisoner. Imagine His heart pounding when they chanted the other prisoner's name, "Barabbas! Barabbas!", over and over again instead of His. When asked about His fate, they screamed out the worse form of punishment that the Romans had to offer, "Crucify Him! Crucify Him!".

The Cross

Imagine the Son of God hanging on a bloody cross. Abandoned by all whom he loved. Rejected by the world He had made. Lied about and laughed at. Humiliated, humbled, cursed and scorned. Every part of His body writhed in tempestuous pain. His hands and feet were bound and pierced. His back was completely torn open by the flagellations of the Roman whip. His eyes stinging from His tears mixed with the blood and sweat from the crown of thorns that He painfully wore. Yet all this would mean nothing because it was His heart that was throbbing and bursting inside.

"My God, my God! Why have You forsaken me?", Jesus screamed through His agony. "Not You too?", He might have thought as the skies grew darker. The Presence that he had always treasured and known from eternity was now slowly stripped away. He was forsaken on that cross by the One who sent Him to become sin for us. On that destined day, the Almighty God turned His gaze away from His Son. It was a necessary wound of the heart and a needful moment of rejection. For without it, not one sin could be atoned for. Not one soul saved. It was the perfect plan of salvation and He was the ultimate sacrifice.

Beloved, make no mistake about it. God and His Son, Jesus Christ, understand our pain. The pain of rejection and broken relationships, loss, and disappointments in life. It was because of that great suffering that He understands us. He knows it all too well. In fact, He still carries in His body the wounds for our healing.

"He is despised and rejected of men; a man of sorrows, and acquainted with grief: and we hid as it were our faces from him; he was despised, and we esteemed him not. Surely he hath borne our grief, and carried our sorrows: yet we did esteem him stricken, smitten of God, and afflicted. But he was wounded for our transgressions, he was bruised for our iniquities: the chastisement of our peace was upon him; and with his stripes we are healed." - Isaiah 53:3-5

Her Work is Done

It was the first day of counseling since Mark's baby girl had died. His thoughts wandered back as his Pastor sat to hear the story. Slowly and thoughtfully, Mark shared the events of the day that changed his life forever.

Taylor Leigh Kenoly was only three months old. He found her cold, lifeless body in her favorite chair that tragic, December morning of 1990. The paramedics worked feverishly to revive her. Sudden Infant Death Syndrome they said. There was shock, confusion, and the screams of Mark's grieving wife in the house that day. He still couldn't believe that she was gone even after all this time. The pain of waking up the morning after and experiencing the demonic grip of self-destructive thoughts. The kingdom of darkness was hovering over the fresh, open wound of Mark's heart like vultures over a bloody carcass.

"I'm gonna hurt somebody or myself", he thought to himself.

It was relentless - the grief from morning until night.

At 9 pm Mark remembered a story he heard in church. How King Jehoshaphat and his army ran to God and praised Him as they went to war. In the midst of their praises, God set an ambush for their enemies and delivered them. In an instant, the guitar was in Mark's hand. He strummed and played every worship song he knew since his conversion three years earlier. Mark worshiped God with every fiber of his being. Then without warning, Mark encountered God's love and grace, shattering the barriers of mourning and grief and started the process of mending his heart and life that night. It was miraculous and supernatural. Jesus, the Anointed One, had begun on that night a three-year process of making Mark's broken heart whole again.

"God didn't take your daughter. But if God received her spirit, it meant that she did everything she was created to do." said his Pastor with compassion afterwards.

Mark agreed. It was illuminating now in hindsight to know that her time was short, but her mission was completed. After the encounter with God that day, Mark has made peace with what happened to his baby girl to begin his path toward healing. Today, he continues to tell her story and the discovery of God's healing presence through praise to bring hope to the hurting as a worship minister of Christ.

The Healer is Waiting

The foundation for recovery from our wounds is found in the Savior, Jesus Christ. He is the Highest Power whereby all men can be saved. He is our Creator. Our Source of life and well-being. He knows us on the inside better than we do and He wants to come into our lives. He's standing at the door of our hearts.

"Behold, I stand at the door, and knock: if any man hear my voice, and open the door, I will come in to him, and will sup with him, and he with me." -Revelation 3:20

Before we go on any further, let me ask you this question– *What are you willing to do to be made whole?* Will you let Christ into your wounded heart? He's the key that unlocks your healing. The medicine that cures the heartache. Will you receive Him as your Healer today? If so, I invite you to open your heart and pray this simple prayer:

"Dear Lord Jesus, come into my heart and life. I need you right now. I'm hurting so much. Heal me, Lord. Make me whole again. Subside the pain and take full control of my life. Forgive me of all my sins, failures and mistakes. I need You in my life and just want to be whole again. Thank you Jesus, for Your mercy and love. I receive You now as my Lord, Savior, and Healer. Amen."

CHAPTER 3

Realize God is Near and Run to Him

"Hear my cry O God; attend unto my prayer. From the end of the
earth will I cry unto Thee, when my heart is overwhelmed:
lead me to the Rock that is higher than I"
-Psalm 61:1-2

I became a follower of Christ in the summer of 1987. Revival had hit the little Church I was attending and it seemed that God was beginning to bring a harvest of souls into that house. It didn't take long though for the enemy to infiltrate the camp. The little flock didn't realize that what started out as a simple disagreement in the leadership became a major fault line separating camps. Fingers started pointing and accusations started flying. The youth were caught in the middle. Our allegiance was torn between the Pastors and the board of Elders, for whom we had much respect.

In the winter of January 1988, things came to a climax. The Pastors resigned their positions and handed over the keys in a tear-filled Sunday morning service. I was a baby Christian, just six months in the Lord. I came to Christ because I saw a love in His people that I had never seen anywhere else. I grew up in a culture that wasn't affectionate and where relationships seemed forced at times. But now, where was this divine love hiding? After the morning service, I stood outside the church as my new friends and church family parted ways. Some were weeping. Others grumbled things with their lips, if not in their heads. I looked at my now ex-youth leader and asked him as I held back the tears, "Why Pastor? We're Christians. It shouldn't be like this!"

With a hesitation, he whispered, "I know. I'm sorry." and he hugged me.

My heart was heavy and burdened. I couldn't understand it. I was only 18 years old and new to this faith. I had given up too much to go back to the world. I was determined to go to another church that evening to find answers.

My First God Encounter

I entered the sanctuary of a local mega church longing for God that night. As the music played, I vowed inwardly to worship God, no matter what.

"I will praise you Father. I've got to. You've got to be real. I'm hurting so bad. How could Your people act like this? No matter what happens, I will worship You. Hallelujah."

In the midst of a worship ballad, God came to me. He heard my cry and saw my heart. It seemed as if all the flood gates holding my tears back were destroyed allowing me to cry uncontrollably. This was no drizzle. It was a monsoon. I cried as I sang my song of praise to Him. Then, it happened. I felt His Presence all around me for the first time. It seemed as if He wrapped His arms around me in a tender embrace. Much like a Father holding his little boy after he had fallen and hurt himself. It made me weep all the more. The more I wept, the more the pain subsided. The more His holy fire burned. His divine love was absorbing and consuming all the hurt and pain out of my weary soul. When He finished 30 minutes later, my heart didn't ache anymore. I had a peace that did surpass all understanding. It was an unforgettable experience. A milestone. An eternal altar built in my mind and heart.

Remember the Altars

On the morning that my ex- fiancée and I broke up, I lay at the altar of the Church I now helped to pastor. I remembered how God had supernaturally healed my broken heart from the church split seven years earlier in that mega church. It happened when I abandoned everything to worship Him. Slowly, I picked myself up from the ground and sat down on the piano bench. I gently lifted the cover and placed my fingers on the ivory keys. I played and sang all the songs I knew in my heart to Him. I cried and sang like the night He first embraced me. I revisited my altar in the wilderness of heartache and again, He came. Only this time, the Lord didn't instantly remove all the hurt as He had previously done. His Presence comforted me just enough to get me on my way to the road of recovery.

God is Near to the Hurting

"The LORD is nigh unto them that are of a broken heart; and saveth such as be of a contrite spirit." -Psalm 34:18

Did you notice the word "nigh" or near in that verse? He promises to be near to those that are of a broken heart. It's ironic. That's when we feel that God is the farthest, but the exact opposite is true. God is not a million miles away. He's the *closest* to us in our heartache.

This is important because when our hearts are broken we genuinely feel that no one cares. That no one understands our pain or sorrow. That there's no one to turn to, but the truth is that God declares that He is near and if we'll reach out to Him, He will surely reach right back. And if God is for us, what can stand against us?

Run to the Lord

"The sacrifices of God are a broken spirit: a broken and a contrite heart, O God, thou wilt not despise." -Psalm 51:17

This is a timeless truth that needs to be understood. God is not interested in any other sacrifice than our hearts. It's the best gift we could ever give to him. Run to God and give Him your heart, even if it's been torn apart. He is a strong tower and refuge. He is a shield and buckler. He is a fortress. In Him we can entrust all the broken pieces of our lives.

Today, we live in a world of choices. There are so many things to run to for comfort or escape from our inward misery. We are all aware of those who have fallen prey to the roaring lion who walks about seeking whom he may devour. It is in our brokenness that we are most vulnerable to temptation. It is no wonder that the devil lures people at this critical juncture in their lives to seek comfort in drugs, alcohol, illicit sex, rebound relationships, food, gaming, gambling, and even shopping. If pleasure is not the hook, then he'll use pain. Anger, vengeance, murder, isolation, and suicide are also works of the devil. *"Anything to fill the void"*, he taunts.

He Left Before His Time

I remembered when he came into my church. He was about 6'2" with shoulder length hair and green eyes. He had on a Hawaiian shirt, pants, and thong slippers. He looked like a hippie and in fact, *he was*. An original one too, from his account. One of the first to gather at Haight and Ashbury in San Francisco in the mid sixties. And now he was a recovering alcoholic and heroin junkie who met Jesus through a local televangelist one night while in a drunken stupor.

"He told me to reach my hand toward the TV screen and pray this prayer. I don't remember what I said, but I know it changed my life. I blacked out after that because I was drunk at the time." said the former hippie.

This dear Brother had a unique way of sharing Christ. He was now in his forties and spent most of his youth as a homeless wino, drug addict and criminal. He had scars on his body to tell the tales of all the car crashes, knife fights and gun barrels that had been aimed at his head. But through it all, he was grateful that God spared his life up to that point so that he could receive Jesus as his personal Savior.

He was now on his fifth year of kicking heroin and alcohol. He spent his days sharing his testimony of how Jesus saved him from the depths of hell on earth. He also became my friend.

In the winter of 1992, his father passed away from a sudden illness. It crushed his spirit.

Within weeks, instead of running to the Lord, he ran to his past.

The old connections. The old habits. The old ways. We saw less of him in church and when he did show up, he seemed dazed and confused, even under the influence. Another minister and I went to his home after a Wednesday night prayer meeting to encourage him. We prayed for him to get rest, but he refused and we sat in his room speechless as he poured out his heart and love for his deceased father.

"Pastor, can you come over? There's something wrong with my son. He's acting up and has locked himself in the bathroom."

Awakened out of sleep by the frantic call from his mother, I glanced at my alarm clock. "Just after 1am", I thought to myself. I hurried over to the house I had left earlier that same evening. It was silent. Strangely silent, even after I had knocked on the door several times. "No one's home. But why? What was that call all about"? I pondered as I sat in my car and began to pray Psalm 91 for God's protection over my friend. It wasn't long before I slowly drifted off to sleep.

"What are you doing here? Show me your driver's license and registration." snapped the police officer as he shined his flashlight to awaken me.

"I was asked to come over by my friend's mother, but when I arrived no one answered the door." I answered respectfully.

Other police officers began to bang on the door. Again, no answer. At this point, his mother arrived home with another relative. She appeared shaken and disturbed.

"We were afraid. He was in a rage, so we left the house.", she said.

As we entered the home, the officers headed straight to the bathroom. They demanded that he open it. Finally, they forced their way in and found him lying on the floor with drug paraphernalia. They tried to revive him, but to no avail. In that moment, he had passed from this life on to the next.

Some would say that he died from a drug overdose or a loss of will to live. I know, however, that he died of a broken heart. The hardest part for me to swallow that night was that *he didn't have to die.*

I believe that he left before his time.

He ran in the wrong direction looking for comfort and healing. He was lied to by the devil! Don't be deceived, friends. The devil and the world have no love for you. The enemy has only three goals in his mind – to steal, kill and destroy. It's his nature, but Jesus promised that He came to give us abundant life.

Only God can Heal a Broken heart

"He healeth the broken in heart, and bindeth up their wounds." *-Psalm 147:3*

In our moments of pain, we all wish there was a miracle pill we could take to fix our broken hearts. The reason a natural or medical solution doesn't exist is that these are matters of the heart and are *spiritual* in nature and only manifest in our emotional and psychological states. Only God who is Spirit can handle and fix spiritual problems.

We take our broken Toyotas to a Toyota Dealer. We take our broken iPhones to the Apple Store. And we should take our broken hearts to the One who made it in the first place. There is much to benefit from the simple phrase "Seek the Lord" that wisely admonishes us so many times in the Scriptures. If more people would do it, I honestly believe that more people would heal from their brokenness and be able to move on with their lives or at the very least find the closure that they so earnestly long for.

God Loves You Eternally

"The LORD hath appeared of old unto me, saying, Yea, I have loved thee with an everlasting love: therefore with lovingkindness have I drawn thee." – Jeremiah 31:3

Here is the most basic of all foundational truths we need to grasp if we are ever going to be truly healed and made whole. We must know and fully understand with every part of our being that we are loved by our great Creator.

The reason we run to the Lord in our pain is not just the fact that He created us and knows how to fix us. It's not really about what He can *do*. It's actually more about who He *is*. We run to Him because we all need *Love*.

Every child has had the experience of hurting themselves and tearfully finding comfort in the arms of a loving parent, relative or guardian. That loving embrace made the emotional pain go away and brought with it a sense of security and comfort – that everything is going to be alright. That's the power of Love over hurt.

"And we have known and believed the love that God hath to us. God is love; and he that dwelleth in love dwelleth in God, and God in him." – I John 4:16

Love heals. Love comforts. Love makes us whole. Love makes us secure and **God is Love**.

His Loving Arms are Wide Open

"Blessed be God, even the Father of our Lord Jesus Christ, the Father of mercies, and the God of all comfort; who comforts us in all our tribulation, that we may be able to comfort them that are in any trouble, by the comfort wherewith we ourselves are comforted of God."
-II Corinthians 1:3-4

He is the God of *all* comfort. There is no lack of peace or satisfaction in Him. He is more than able to deliver us from the afflictions of the heart. He has promised to never leave us or forsake us. He'll make time for us any time of the day. He's available and His arms are open wide. He is with us to the end of the world. His steadfast love extends to the heavens. His faithfulness to the depths of the sea. His loving-kindness endures to all generations. Thank God He's not afar off, but near, and *nearest* to those who are of a broken heart. So if you're going to run for comfort, be wise and run to God the Healer.

A sample prayer to set yourself to run to God for healing:

"Heavenly Father, I give you my broken heart. I give You all the pieces that it has shattered into. I ask that You would mend it and put it back together again. I seek You for my inner healing, From this moment on, You are my peace. My contentment and my source of life and joy. Let my healing begin now. Make me completely whole again. I thank You for your great love for me. Let me find comfort now knowing that You are with me and will finish this work that You have begun in me. In Jesus' name, amen."

CHAPTER 4

See the Big Picture. God is Still in Control.

"Trust in the Lord with all thine heart and lean not unto thine own understanding. In all thy ways acknowledge Him and He shall direct thy paths."
-Proverbs 3:5-6

I asked the Lord one night, why my seven year relationship ended and Proverbs 3:5 came to mind. I felt that He was asking me to trust Him with my whole life even though that season of it was very painful. That simple, yet powerful verse saved my life and anchored me for a year and a half. Truthfully, I was having difficulty praying and reading the Bible. My emotions were running wild, my thoughts were cloudy, and I didn't have any desire to read and study the Word except for that one passage. I couldn't read anything else. That Scripture sustained and upheld me for over a year!

Most of that time, I was in a state of confusion. I spent large amounts of time driving around at night and praying and crying out to God. I would look up into the starry night sky and invoke God for my inner healing. My heart hurt every day, and I mean *every* single day.

This verse helped me to understand that God had a *path* for me. We were on a journey together and only He knew the way. I was a passenger in His vehicle of life and I had to trust Him wholeheartedly. He had a destination and I had a destiny. What happened to me was just a stumbling block after leaving point A, but it definitely wasn't point B yet.

One of the hardest things to do is trust God with our whole hearts. Our human nature wants total control. We need to know everything so we can handle every situation. But let's face it, He's God. We're just mere mortals apart from Him. A wisp of smoke that appears for a little while and then vanishes away. He sees the big picture because He's a big God and has a much higher point of view.

Fly Higher

Have you ever been in a traffic jam? I mean a good rush hour traffic jam? It's frustrating at times because you can't see *why* it's bumper to bumper traffic. All you can see is the car in front of you. But imagine if you were in a helicopter and flying *above* the traffic. In that flying machine, you could see the *cause* of the traffic jam and how far it stretches ahead of your car.

Life is a bit like that. We're here on earth and it's difficult to see the road ahead because of all the trials and hurts in life that we experience. They seem to have power to block our progress and slow our journey. When we encounter them, it's hard to see what good the future holds. God, however, isn't bound to earth. The earth is His footstool. Heaven is where His throne is and from way up there, He can see everything. The causes of our problems and the road that lies ahead of us. That's why we can't lean or rely upon our own understanding of the circumstances. We may interpret the facts wrong. We need to see things from our Heavenly Father's exalted perspective.

Father Knows Best

"Are not two sparrows sold for a farthing? and one of them shall not fall on the ground without your Father. But the very hairs of your head are all numbered. Fear ye not therefore, ye are of more value than many sparrows." -Matthew 10:29-31

Can you see it? God knows everything. It's reassuring to know that He hasn't forgotten about us, especially in our times of sorrow and brokenness. We're more important to Him than the sparrows. He knows every strand of hair on our head and everything that's going on inside of us too. He knows why we hurt and how to fix it. He knows us by name. The Bible declares that He knew us before we were even in our mother's womb (Jeremiah 1:5).

Let Wisdom Speak

"My brethren, count it all joy when ye fall into divers temptations... If any of you lack wisdom, let him ask of God, that giveth to all men liberally, and upbraideth not; and it shall be given him." -James 1:2,5

There is always a reason why everything happens. God is omniscient. Nothing escapes His notice. The darkness is light to Him. James promises in that verse that God will enlighten every situation with wisdom if we ask him to. When God speaks, we'll see that there is a *revelation in every situation*. We may not understand it immediately because it's beyond our control, but it's never beyond the reach of God's understanding or grasp. His illumination in our circumstances will bring life to us. When the Father reveals truth, it causes us to see things from His perspective. There is a bigger picture. If we ask Him in simple faith, He'll show it unto us.

Zoom Out

"Sometimes you can't see the forest through the trees." -Unknown

You may have heard this quote at some point in your life. Its truth is actually timeless. Sometimes, we focus in on something too much and miss what we were supposed to see. When we're hurting, sometimes that hurt is all we can think of or talk about. That's understandable, but when it becomes the *only* thing we live for, then we've hindered our emotional recovery. Let's take another illustration from the film industry.

Imagine that your life is like a great movie (you know, the ones that make you cry and laugh at the same time). Your suffering is just one scene from the film, but it doesn't tell the whole story. There's still a climax and an ending to bring closure to it. God is the Writer and Director and He always sends the Director's cut to be released to the public. In any great film, there is an intro, a hero and a villain, heartache and laughter, and some form of enlightenment in the end. Everything makes sense and everything works out. Life is not a fairy tale, but it doesn't have to be a tragedy either, especially for those who trust in God.

So let the Great Director zoom out and show you the panoramic view of your life. It may be a jungle out there, but at least you can now see the forest instead of the trees. Believe me, bigger is better in this instance.

God Loves Great Endings

"Likewise the Spirit also helpeth our infirmities: for we know not what we should pray for as we ought: but the Spirit itself maketh intercession for us with groanings which cannot be uttered. And He that searcheth the hearts knoweth what is the mind of the Spirit, because He maketh intercession for the saints according to the will of God. And we know that all things work together for good to them that love God, to them who are the called according to His purpose." -Romans 8:26-28

This Scripture promises a good conclusion and a greater purpose for those who belong to the Lord. Some people might get upset at this, but the truth is that God loves great endings. That's what hope is for. Hope means that you're expecting something good to come out of every circumstance. That your tomorrow will be much better than today. He is the God of all hope and hope is the foundation of faith.

If we'll realize that God is in control and we trust Him to take care of us, then we can expect things to work out for our good. He has great plans for us – plans for our benefit and not our destruction. Jesus can save those who come unto Him and He is able to do exceedingly, abundantly above all that we can ask or even think. Let's learn to trust

Him with all our hearts and lean less unto our own understanding. Let's ask Him to show us the big picture in spite of our hurts and the wisdom to correctly interpret our circumstances.

Reunited and It Feels so Good

In the summer of 1975, my family arrived on the shores of the United States of America. Refugees of war they called us. Our family barely escaped the fall of Saigon, Vietnam a few months earlier. My father was a Naval officer for the Southern Vietnamese military. My mother was an English interpreter at the time. They courted through letters for a season and married in 1968. I was born a year later– the first of four children during the Vietnam war.

Coming to America was a difficult transition for my parents. A new culture, language, and community. Still, they made the best of things as we settled first in Willmar, Minnesota through the kindness of a Lutheran Church that was adopting refugee families. Three years later, our family moved to San Jose, California in the spring of 1978. Both of my parents worked odd jobs to make ends meet. Eventually, they migrated into the blossoming technology field. It was the humble beginnings of the Silicon Valley.

Gradually, my parents began to grow distant. It became painfully obvious that they were exact opposites. My father was social and outgoing. My mother was quiet and stoic. After the purchase of our first house, it seemed that we were starting to live out the American Dream. How quickly dreams change.

By 1982, the dream became a nightmare. My parents filed for divorce and the family split up. My brother and I lived with my father. My two sisters lived with my mother. I rarely ever saw them during my teenage years. The holidays were not the same. Birthdays and other social events that would signify joy for a healthy family were a burden for ours. My father was heartbroken and we became statistics for the rising divorce rate.

By the time I graduated from high school, I had met the Lord. My parents had moved on with their lives, or so it seemed. My father was considering remarriage and my mother was pursuing her growing career. Yet inside, I couldn't help but wish that by some miracle of God, He would put my family back together again. Like any child from a divorced home, I prayed for that miracle to occur.

Four years later, even after my father did remarry and my mother had moved on with her life, God intervened! I don't know how or why, but He remembered my prayers. My father's second marriage failed and my mother was still single in the fall of 1991. They had little communication since their divorce nine years earlier, but somehow my father managed the courage to call my mother to reconcile and she accepted.

I came home one evening to see my mother in the hallway of the house she left nine years earlier. I was in utter shock.

"Mom, what are you doing here?"

"I went out with your Dad." She replied with a smile. Within moments, my father appeared from his master bedroom.

"Hi son! Your mom and I are spending time together."

My heart was beating like a taiko drum. I was witnessing a miracle of God. The prayers of my youth were now being answered before my eyes. I had given up on that heartfelt prayer when my father married his second wife, but God didn't. He was faithful, oh so faithful.

My parents remarried in the first month of the new year. We became a family again after ten long years of divorce.

In our case, things did work out for good in the end. They are still married today over twenty years later, and every time I see them, I see the hand of a miraculous and loving God.

A sample prayer to see the big picture in life:

"Heavenly Father, I ask that you grant me the eyes to see what You see for my life. It's hard for me to see clearly in my pain right now, but I trust You and ask that You open my eyes. Help me to see the big picture and not to stay so focused on this painful episode of life. I thank You now for the hope of a brighter and better tomorrow. In Jesus' name, amen."

CHAPTER 5

Get Better. Not Bitter.

"Humble yourselves therefore under the mighty hand of God,
that he may exalt you in due time: Casting all your care
upon him; for he careth for you."
-I Peter 5:6-7

Give God your pain in prayer. Open up your heart to Him and be totally honest. Share your anger, disappointment, frustration and hurt. Tell Him that you're upset and ask Him to listen to your side of the story. You're not telling Him something he doesn't *already* know.

We've got to stop trying to hide behind our masks and let the truth be known before God. The Apostle Peter exhorted us to "cast all our care upon Him". All means all. No exceptions. If you want to fully recover from heartache, you've got to fully release everything to God. He wants it all.

I have to be totally honest with you though. It won't happen overnight. You'll have to keep giving it to God every time it affects you negatively in any way. At times, this could be a daily affair. Don't let the frequency of the flashbacks deter you though. Keep casting your cares upon Him. Another word for *cast* is to *throw. Keep throwing that pain God's way.* He doesn't mind it. He can handle infinitely more than we can. The weakness of God will always be stronger than the strongest of men.

God is not too busy to help you. It's interesting that I hear this excuse from time to time as to why people don't ask God for help. They feel that He's too busy running the universe to help them work through their pain. The Scriptures reveal that God gave His Son to die a painful death so that we could live an eternally joyful life. Anything that robs us of the joy that He already paid for is an enemy to His finished work on Calvary's cross. So just do it. Give Him that world of hurt today and free yourself.

Choose You This Day Whom You'll Forgive

"For if you forgive men their trespasses, your heavenly Father will also forgive you: But if you forgive not men their trespasses, neither will your Father forgive your trespasses." -Matthew 6:14-15

One of the hardest things to do when someone has taken our hearts and trampled on it is to forgive them. They don't deserve it. Not one ounce of our forgiveness. However, according to this excerpt from the Lord's teaching on prayer, the forgiveness is not really for their benefit. *It's for ours.*

In order to get better, we must learn how to stop ourselves from being bitter. The only difference between the words better and bitter is the big "I" in the middle.

Can "I" forgive or not?

This is where the heart of the matter lies. It's one of the biggest stumbling blocks to the healing of the wounded heart. Sometimes, because of a stubborn disposition, many just adamantly refuse to forgive, thereby throwing away the key to their healing.

"No way! Uh-uh. Not in a million years. When hell freezes over!", they'll say. Forgiveness, however, begins with a choice. A choice to heal and move forward with life. That can only happen when we're willing to let go of the hurt and the people who may have caused it.

Why Dig Two Graves?

There's a Chinese proverb that illustrates the effects of unforgiveness. It says, "When you seek vengeance, dig two graves." It's just a fancy way of saying that if we don't forgive, we're heading to the same grave they are. Jesus clearly said that God will not forgive us if we do not forgive others. No forgiveness from God equals little chance of blessing and even a lower chance of entrance into heaven. It's that simple. Make a choice to forgive the ones who broke your heart and set *yourself* free! The parable in Matthew chapter eighteen illustrates this principle:

"Then came Peter to him, and said, Lord, how oft shall my brother sin against me, and I forgive him? till seven times? Jesus saith unto him, I say not unto thee, Until seven times: but, Until seventy times seven. Therefore is the kingdom of heaven likened unto a certain king, which would take account of his servants. And when he had begun to reckon, one was brought unto him, which owed him ten thousand talents. But forasmuch as he had not to pay, his lord commanded him to be sold, and his wife, and children, and all that he had, and payment to be made. The servant therefore fell down, and worshipped him, saying, Lord, have patience with me, and I will pay thee all. Then the lord of that servant was moved with compassion, and loosed him, and forgave him the debt. But the same servant went out, and found one of his fellowservants, which owed him an hundred pence: and he laid hands on him, and took him by the throat, saying, Pay me that thou owest. And his fellowservant fell down at his feet, and besought him, saying, Have patience with me, and I will pay thee all. And he would not: but went and cast him into prison, till he should pay the debt. So when his fellowservants saw what was done, they were very sorry, and came and told unto their lord all that was done. Then his lord, after that he had called him, said unto him, O thou wicked servant, I forgave thee all that debt, because thou desiredst me: Shouldest not thou also have had compassion on thy fellowservant, even as I had pity on thee? And his lord was wroth, and delivered him to the tormentors, till he

should pay all that was due unto him. So likewise shall my heavenly Father do also unto you, if ye from your hearts forgive not every one his brother their trespasses." -Matthew 18:21-35

The steward imprisoned himself when he didn't forgive like his master. Forgiveness is a very serious matter and one in which we need the Lord's help to do it.

I remember I had to make that difficult decision with my ex-fiancée. I was angry and growing bitter. I was starting to have thoughts like, *"All women are the same. They just want to break your heart"*. I was afraid that I was starting to become a woman-hater. I was afraid that my anger would overcome my reason and common sense. I knew it was not a true statement, but it was an expression of my heart at the time– a heart that was broken and bleeding.

Does this sound familiar? There are people we all know who put others into a box and label everyone the same. It's usually the people that they associate with their past hurts and wounds. It's the subconscious projection of our inner wounds that never healed correctly onto another person. This allows the unforgiveness to form a root of bitterness. Then once bitterness forms, it's like a weed that isn't so easily uprooted and will form the lenses by which we view the world and those around us. Bitterness can even blind us to the ones that truly do love us and are trying to help.

It's a Heart Thing

Roots of bitterness often bear fruit in the words that people speak. In my case, my anger toward my ex-fiancée was starting to express itself in my thought life and eventually in my statements. I thank God that He gave me the grace to forgive and not hold a grudge against my former fiancée and women in general.

It's common though for us to hear things like:

"All men are dogs."

"All Christians are hypocrites."

"All salespeople are con artists."

"All politicians are liars."

"All women are gold-diggers."

Please don't misunderstand my message. There *are* people who are like that. But not *all* of them are like that.

It's obvious that when these type of statements are spoken by an individual or group, they reveal an unresolved hurt or issue that needs to be dealt with and where true forgiveness needs to be applied. There's plenty of hate to go around, but as those made in the image and likeness of God, we must not be overcome by evil, but learn to overcome evil with good. If you want to know where people are and how their hearts are doing, just listen to what they have to say.

"...for out of the abundance of the heart the mouth speaketh." *-Matthew 12:34*

You Have the Power

Now it's up to you. You have the God-given right and authority to forgive the ones who've hurt you. God will give you the grace and strength to do it, but the choice is yours. He made His choice to forgive us when we didn't deserve it, and He expects the same from us for others who don't deserve it.

Remember that even on the cross surrounded by those who betrayed Him and wanted Him dead, Jesus uttered the most profound statement on forgiveness:

"Then said Jesus, Father, forgive them; for they know not what they do. And they parted his raiment, and cast lots." *-Luke 23:34*

His decision to forgive that day forever changed our standing before God. God forgives. Christ forgives. We can do the same by His grace and mercy.

As I mentioned previously, this will not be a onetime decision nor will it happen overnight. We'll have to make this choice every moment of our lives or as long as it takes for us to be truly whole again. Sometimes we have to choose forgiveness when we wake up and when we lie down. Other times it's when we see those who've done us wrong around town, work, school, church or even home. We can either let them dictate how we feel for the rest of our lives or seize the day, and take our lives back. That includes our joy, our peace, and our sanity.

My Decision to Get Better

I made that choice to forgive. I knew that if I didn't do it, I was jeopardizing my life, my call, and my destiny. It was for *my benefit* that I forgave her, and I still do forgive her. Whenever the thought of what happened enters into my mind, even to this day, I say out loud, "I forgive so and so!" and move on. I don't dwell there. I go on. That's part of forgiveness. We've got to release it and then move on with life. This is how we get better.

Being "Better" means that we are not in the same place that we were before. It means that we've grown. It means that we've improved in some way. It means that we're now free from the things that once oppressed us and held us back. One of the best examples in the modern age of choosing to get better instead of bitter is the former President of South Africa, Nelson Mandela.

A Decision That Changed a Nation

Nelson Mandela served 27 years in prison for being an activist against apartheid (racial discrimination) in South Africa. When they finally released him after almost three decades, he made a decision that would make history and change his nation to this day:

"As I walked out the door toward the gate that would lead to my freedom, I knew if I didn't leave my bitterness and hatred behind, I'd still be in prison."

Mandela knew that if he was to bring reconciliation between the races living in the nation of South Africa, it had to start in *him*. He chose the path of forgiveness and left bitterness behind. His desire to create a better nation helped him become South Africa's first Black African President and awarded him a Nobel Peace Prize. He made life better for his people because he was made better by that decision to forgive. Forgiveness is never an easy decision, but it's a powerful decision that will affect everyone and everything around us.

If you're ready to make that decision to forgive the ones that have hurt you and move on with your life, then pray this with me. This prayer is not a magic formula. It's just a vehicle for you to express your innermost desires to God. You can use your own words if you want, but make sure you release all the people who've hurt you once and for all.

A sample prayer to forgive those who've hurt us:

"Heavenly Father, I'm ready to forgive all the people who have hurt me. I do this not because they all deserve it, but because I need it. With your help, I now forgive (name their names) and release them from all the hurt, all the pain, all the anguish and disappointment they have caused me. I now give them over to You and trust You to handle things from now on. Heal me of all my anger and bitterness. I just want to get better in Jesus' Name. Amen."

CHAPTER 6

Come Against the Force of Shame

"Confess your faults one to another, and pray one for another,
that ye may be healed. The effectual fervent prayer of
a righteous man availeth much."
-James 5:16

James the Elder tells us that confession is a precursor to healing. In other words, get things off your chest if you want the prayers of healing to be effective. Talk, talk, and talk about what happened to you. Bring it into the light by your honesty. The devil works in the darkness where things are unconfessed. Render him powerless through your confession before God and men.

I've noticed a common thread among those who experience heartbreak. There's usually a strong sense of shame that comes upon us. It causes us to retreat into a cave and become hermits. We isolate ourselves and are reluctant to admit that we're hurting even when concerned family and friends begin to inquire. This sense of shame makes us believe that silence is the best route to inner peace when it's actually causing us to go in the opposite direction. It's difficult to heal when we aren't willing to open up and talk about things. If we do break the silence, it's to mumble excuses that mask the truth about how we're really hurting inside.

"It's cool...I'll be just fine."

Imagine for humor's sake, if we can translate that into heartbreak language: "It's cool...like the icepack on my swollen heart.", "I'm OK...actually, more like KO'd.", and "I'll be just fine...after my emotional morphine shots."

Don't ignore and repress the pain inside. Face it and share it. It's a humbling experience to talk about how hurt you are. Humility allows the grace of God to work, but pride is what keeps it away.

My Little Secret

I remembered announcing to my coworkers at the advertising agency where I worked at the time that I had just been engaged. They were ecstatic for me. Now, six months later, I was single again. Believe me, I was ashamed to admit that the whole thing failed. I didn't want anyone to know that my dreams were shattered and I was a broken man. I kept up the façade. Day in. Day out. I was determined that no one would know what had happened. I was determined to be strong no matter what. I kept conversations about my supposed upcoming marriage low key, but all the while inside, I was falling apart.

It was starting to affect me at church too. I was an Assistant Pastor and Pastors have an image to upkeep I naively believed. "After all, we're the examples of the Lord. ", I repeatedly told myself. I was living in delusion and my world was crumbling. It wasn't until I couldn't hold it inside any longer that I sought to find someone to confide in.

It was then that I remembered my dear friend and music minister, Mark Kenoly and his testimony of God's grace to help him overcome the pain of his baby daughter's death. "If anyone knows heartache, it's Mark. I know he'll understand", I thought to myself.

As Mark and I sat in his home music studio, I began to open up and confide in him. I told him of my anger, resentment, hurt and pain. I was disappointed and weary of holding a front for ministry's sake.

It was then that Mark gave me this liberating principle that I'm sharing with you.

"You need to talk about it. Come against the force of *shame*. Tell as many people as you can to release it. It will be difficult at first, but gradually over time and repeatedly sharing your story, the pain will begin to subside. That's what happened with me." said Mark confidently.

Needless to say, I took his advice and began to work out my healing with God's help. The next day, I came into work and determined to unmask the lie and break the shame off myself. I sat at my terminal and sent a company-wide email letting everyone know that my fiancée and I had broken up. It was over and there was going to be no reconciliation. Within, hours, letters of sympathy and condolences came back. It seemed as if a huge weight had been lifted from my being. Next step, was telling my church family.

I planned to tell the people in my small church individually. This was much more difficult since my ex-fiancée used to attend with me, but the more I confessed it, the better I felt on the inside. Just like my coworkers before them, the people of God extended their love and comfort toward me. I was thankful and relieved to finally get the truth out and allow the inner healing of Christ to begin.

"An open confession is good for the soul" – Scottish proverb

We must learn to fight the shame that keeps our mouths shut. Fight the pride that wants to present a perfect image every time. Learn to openly confess those hurts and get them off our chests. This allows people in to support us on our journey of healing.

God wants truth in our inward parts. Don't repress those painful feelings. Let God in on it. All that rage, frustration, anger, and pain will eventually come out one way or another. Deal with them now, by pouring out our hearts to God and men. It's good for the soul.

Imitate the Children

Have you ever seen how children deal with hurt? I remember one day in front of my parents' house a few years ago seeing my neighbor teach her child how to walk. She lovingly placed the little girl on her two feet, on the sidewalk, and then slowly took two steps back. I saw the fear, hurt, and anguish in that little girl's face as the security of her mother's embrace was stripped from her. Do you know what that little girl did? She did *not* take a step toward her mother first. The first thing she did was scream at the top of her little lungs! When she did, her mother immediately reacted and took a step toward the girl. When she saw her mother coming toward her, then she bravely took some of her first steps.

We can learn so much from little children. They certainly get the help they need because they are vocal about it. The first gift God gives a baby in need is the ability to open its mouth. When they're hungry, they cry. When they're sleepy, they cry. When they're sick, they cry. You get the idea. Children are not afraid to open their mouths. Jesus, who loved to bless the children, said that we must be like them to enter God's Kingdom – a Kingdom of righteousness, peace, and joy in the Holy Spirit.

The King's Memoirs

Of all the Books of the Bible, it seems that the Psalms are unanimously the favorite for comfort and consolation by most Christians. Most of the Psalms were written by King David through the anointing of the Holy Spirit. David, himself, was no stranger to brokenness and heartache. Hounded by the king he vowed to serve, he wandered in the caves, mountains, and wilderness for years. It was there that he experienced the Lord as his constant companion, shepherd, and friend.

What makes the Psalms so powerful are the ways in which David expressed how he *honestly felt* at each season of his life. They are an expression of his innermost feelings and a personal memoir of his cries to God for help in the midst of his struggles.

"How long wilt thou forget me, O LORD? Forever? How long wilt Thou hide thy face from me? How long shall I take counsel in my soul, having sorrow in my heart daily? how long shall mine enemy be exalted over me? Consider and hear me, O LORD my God: lighten mine eyes, lest I sleep the sleep of death; Lest mine enemy say, I have prevailed against him; and those that trouble me rejoice when I am moved. But I have trusted in Thy mercy; my heart shall rejoice in Thy salvation. I will sing unto the LORD, because He hath dealt bountifully with me." -Psalm 13

David was not afraid to tell God how he felt. We must break away from a religious attitude and get honest with God. Remember, God looks at our hearts before He even hears our words. Don't ignore how you feel. Talk about it even if it hurts and one day, the pain will subside.

A suggested prayer for the courage to share your pain with others:

"Heavenly Father, I ask that You give me the courage to open up and share my pain. Help me not to keep it all inside, but to release it first to You and then a close confidant. I pray that I receive the healing that You promised for all those who confess their pain and that I can obtain the peace I've been longing for, for so long. In Jesus' name I thank You, amen."

CHAPTER 7

Reach for Tomorrow

*"Where there is no vision, the people perish: but he that
keepeth the law, happy is he."*
-Proverbs 29:18

What do you want for your tomorrow?

I knew what I wanted - to stop hurting, to get help, and to find some hope for my future. If this sounds like you, then smile because that's good news. You have some goals to work toward in life and that's a good thing.

Goals are what keep us future oriented instead of past oriented. It's important to know that we have something to live for in the midst of all the hurt and pain we are dealing with in the present. Our future hopes are what keep us alive. The Bible is clear in declaring that without a vision (goal or dream), people perish.

The world is filled with people who have given up on life and don't want to go on anymore because they feel they have nothing to live for. When you have nothing to live for, you are *dying* inside. I've ministered to people from all walks of life who can only focus on that one past event in their lives that broke them as people. When they recount their stories of bitterness and loss, it seems as if they are reliving that moment right there and then.

Please don't misunderstand me. Looking toward the future does not mean that we ignore the past and act as if it never happened.

Neither is making the choice to move forward with our healing, especially if we're mourning the loss of a loved one, an indicator that we'll no longer remember them in our future. Rather, it means that we're willing to deal with the past, and after dealing with it, we diligently move forward with the life that we have been given. If we've lost a loved one, it means that we choose to live a full life in honor of their blessed memory. This is a choice that only you and I can make. No one can make this decision for us. We must choose to release the pain of our past in order to embrace the possibilities of our future.

Only we can check ourselves out of heartbreak hotel. Matters of the heart are very sensitive and personal. No matter how much others want for us to be healed, the decision to move forward with our recovery is ours alone. However, when we do make that decision to reach for tomorrow, nothing can stop us from making progress.

Sometimes we have to do this without proper closure. There may never be an apology for us or we may not get the chance to make matters right. Maybe those who've hurt us have passed away or want nothing to do with us. The power of reaching for tomorrow is that it starts to move us away from the epicenter of our pain and allows God to begin His healing work within us.

Head Back to the Future

"For I know the thoughts that I think toward you, saith the LORD, thoughts of peace, and not of evil, to give you an expected end."
-Jeremiah 29:11

The future is bright with God at our side. He tells the nation of Israel that He has thoughts of peace and not evil toward them. If God has good thoughts for a nation whom He calls His people, how much more for those that He calls His own children?

Remember, hope is the expectation of good things in the future, i.e. a good ending. God, our Father, has great plans for us to give us hope. They are beyond what we can see, hear, or even understand at this present moment. Pursuing God's plans for the future is like driving a car to get to our favorite destination. No one drives forward looking in the rear view mirror! It's the same with life. We can't move forward always looking at the past. Keep your eyes on the road ahead of you. Step on the pedal and leave Painesville and Heartbreak Hotel behind. We only get one life so why waste it?

Time only moves one way – forward. Our minds want to live in the moment of our pain. Fight that urge and declare that you will not waste another moment thinking about the past and putting your life in neutral or on hold. Get yourself in gear and head toward your destiny – God's appointed calling and destination.

Saved By the Call

I remember that immediately after my break-up, my world spun into a haze of confusion. It was difficult to focus on anything. But there was one thing that kept me going and looking at my future – the call of God on my life.

I knew that I was called to the ministry and that one day I was going to preach the gospel all over the world.

I knew that I would one day become a Senior Pastor and build a strong local Church.

It came down to a decision – either leave all this pain behind and go for the future God had prepared for me or put my life on "pause" and throw in the towel. The painful memories gripped me daily, but I knew I had to move forward. My destiny was calling me.

I think I made the second most important decision of my life at that crucial point (the first was to receive Christ). I decided to pursue God and His high calling and to never look back no matter what it cost me. I made a decision to put all of my strength, heart, and soul into my dreams of ministry and to stop wasting time and energy lamenting the past. It was onward and upward from that moment on.

Day Dream Believer

Maybe the words vision, goal, or even the future seem like some distant universe to you. Another way to look at the future is to focus on your *dreams*. In the last chapter, we talked about learning from children. If there's one thing about kids I love, it's their ability to day dream and talk about their futures with earnest enthusiasm.

Do you remember when you were a child? You may have said things like, "When I grow up..." or "I can't wait until I'm...". These are expressions of hope, an expectation of good things in the future. When we said those things, we were in a future oriented state. Our lives were lived preparing for our futures. Our schooling and education was to prepare us for the future. We don't have to lose that just because we're adults now. In fact, we have something more powerful now than we did in our childhood – the ability and resources to act on those dreams.

Don't stop dreaming and don't stop pursuing your dreams.

Mark up your calendar. Plan some activities. Here are some pursuits worth considering:

1. Focus on a career path to climb the corporate ladder.

2. Get your high school or college degree.

3. Start that business you've always envisioned.

4. Take that dream vacation.

5. Go on that missions trip.

6. Fall in love or marry the love of your life.

7. Spend time with old friends or make new ones.

8. Choose to laugh…a lot.

9. Create new and good memories.

10. Spend more time on that hobby.

11. Learn a new skill, activity, or gain a new experience.

12. Start that ministry or charity.

The list could go on forever, but the point is to do things that will get you future oriented.

Remember, you can't change your past, but you can shape your future by making a decision to do something with it today.

"Brethren, I count not myself to have apprehended: but this one thing I do, forgetting those things which are behind, and reaching forth unto those things which are before, I press toward the mark for the prize of the high calling of God in Christ Jesus." -Philippians 3:13-14

If you're ready to embrace a bright future today, here is a suggested prayer for vision in your life:

"Dear Heavenly Father, I ask that you help me to focus on my purpose and destiny in life. With Your help, I choose to believe that life will get better and that I will heal from this heartache. I thank You for giving me a vision for my life and the courage to pursue it. May all my dreams come true. In Jesus' name, amen."

CHAPTER 8

Find Somebody to Love

"Even as the Son of man came not to be ministered unto,
but to minister, and to give his life a ransom for many."
-Matthew 20:28

L et's stop for a moment. Up to this point, we've been talking about *our* wounds and *our* broken hearts. But what if we shifted the focus off of ourselves and onto those around us? I know what some of you are thinking, "But if I'm hurting, how can I help someone else?." By the same power that will heal you– the grace of God! Jesus declared that He came to help and serve others and not the other way around. He's the same yesterday, today, and forever and He lives in everyone who confesses Him as Lord and Savior. If this is you, then rise up because Jesus wants to live big in you to reach those around you. In fact, sometimes we focus too much on ourselves and our pain that we can't see any other way out. The only solution for this is to stop looking at yourself and do what Jesus did – go serve someone and make their day. In the end, it will make yours.

Avoid the Black Hole Syndrome

Many years ago, scientists were amazed to find that there were areas in space with gravitational pulls so strong that not even light could escape it. Fascinated, they discovered that these black holes were once light bearing stars whose gravitational pull inward was so strong that it caused the star to collapse, sucking all the light inward into a vast dark hole in the blanket of space.

This is a great illustration from creation of what can happen when we focus on ourselves too much. Becoming self-absorbed can be dangerous over a prolonged period of time. All the light of God in our lives can be sucked into that cold, dark area called pain and we can lose our brilliance and will to live.

Depression, suicidal tendencies, and isolation are sometimes caused by focusing on our wounds until it becomes a mountain so high that we can't climb over it anymore. This is where some give up. But the truth is, it doesn't have to be this way.

We have a word for this type of behavior, *self-pity*, and it's never benefited anyone. Resist it at all costs. It will kill your joy and keep you to a slave to pain. It will make you a hermit and an island to the ones you love and who love you.

Refuse to see yourself as the victim, but rather the victor over life's circumstances and events. The Bible declares that we are "more than conquerors" and "victorious in Christ Jesus"! Let's believe what God says about us more than the memories of our past.

What Goes Around…Comes Around

There is a spiritual law in God's Kingdom called the law of sowing and reaping. What you want to receive, you must be willing to give away. In nature, if you want apples, you must plant apple seeds. In life, if you want to reap love, you must plant the seeds of love. If you want to receive joy, go find someone to sow joy into!

Our Heavenly Father operates in this law all the time. God never waits for anyone or anything to get what He wants. He's an initiator! We love Him because He *first* loved us! He gave us His only begotten Son *before* any of us ever became His sons or daughters. He reached out to us before we ever sought Him. We can do the same because He lives in us. Don't let anything stand in your way. Refuse to give up on being whole again. Go get what belongs to you!

"Be not deceived; God is not mocked: for whatsoever a man soweth, that shall he also reap." -Galatians 6:7

Did you notice the word "whatsoever"? It means *whatever* we sow, we will also reap. It is commonly used to warn people in the areas of destructive behavior, but the Apostle Paul used the word "whatsoever" so that can mean good things too.

If you sow to the Spirit of Life, you will reap everlasting life. If you want to find peace in your heart again, make peace with someone. If you want to be happy, be determined to make someone else happy. Look at it as an opportunity to plant something good so you can reap something good.

During my prolonged journey toward healing, the Holy Spirit reminded me of this Kingdom principle. I took it as sound advice and started writing songs to bless people. Back then, I recorded them on simple cassette tapes and then I gave them away. The songs were from the Lord and they started making people happy. I knew that my sowing would pay off later. I even went a step further and invested into some Christian t-shirts. I designed them myself and then gave them away. I went out and found people to sow into. Thank God, my harvest did come. The Father gave back to me what money could not buy – a mended heart.

Living to Give and Giving to Live

Something else powerful happens when we sow into the lives of others. We start to build meaning into our own existence. We realize that our lives do matter. That we are not as independent as we thought. We're not trees that fall in the forest without anyone hearing. What we do does have meaning. Our lives are important to God and others. We are are genuinely needed. This makes life a precious, heaven-sent gift and one worth living in spite of its ups and downs.

It's interesting to note that the two greatest commandments according to Jesus Christ in Mark 12:30-31 are 1) to love God with all our heart, soul, mind, and strength, and 2) to love our neighbor as we love ourselves.

These commandments have everything to do with what we can give away to God and others. They are outward-focused acts. In other words, they represent a life that is always giving on purpose.

In fact, the whole point of our journey is to give everything away until our last breath on earth. It is like what Paul described about his life in his last letter to Timothy, *"For I am now ready to be offered, and the time of my departure is at hand."* -II Timothy 4:6

He saw his life as an offering to God that was poured out until there was nothing left. I know that some will think, "If I give everything away, I'll have nothing left and as it is, I don't have much to give after what happened to me!" That's not what Jesus thinks. He said that if we lose our lives for His sake and the gospel, we will gain it again! If you give of yourself, you'll *regain* your life! Don't lose heart. Don't give up. You will get your life back. Just be willing to give and it will be given back to you in a *"...good measure, pressed down, and shaken together, and running over, shall men give into your bosom..."* (Luke 6:38).

Through your giving, you will gain a sense of self-worth and confidence. You will feel needed and a part of something greater than yourself, which is important to anyone recovering from a broken heart.

It's a Wonderful Life

Did you know that the word "blessed" also means to be "happy" or one whose life is "to be envied"? When our hearts are broken, happiness seems like a distant fantasy on the other side of the universe. It's on the exact opposite end of the spectrum from sorrow. Yet, again, Jesus Christ taught His disciples the benefit of giving – a state of blessedness or happiness. A wonderful life, if you will.

Let's consider this principle on the night of Jesus' betrayal and the saddest night of His earthly life, Jesus did something remarkable after the last supper.

"Jesus knowing that the Father had given all things into his hands, and that he was come from God, and went to God; He riseth from supper, and laid aside his garments; and took a towel, and girded himself. After that he poureth water into a bason, and began to wash the disciples' feet, and to wipe them with the towel wherewith he was girded. Then cometh he to Simon Peter: and Peter saith unto him, Lord, dost thou wash my feet? Jesus answered and said unto him, What I do thou knowest not now; but thou shalt know hereafter. Peter saith unto him, Thou shalt never wash my feet. Jesus answered him, If I wash thee not, thou hast no part with me. Simon Peter saith unto him, Lord, not my feet only, but also my hands and my head. Jesus saith to him, He that is washed needeth not save to wash his feet, but is clean every whit: and ye are clean, but not all. For he knew who should betray him; therefore said he, Ye are not all clean. So after he had washed their feet, and had taken his garments, and was set down again, he said unto them, Know ye what I have done to you? Ye call me Master and Lord: and ye say well; for so I am. If I then, your Lord and Master, have washed your feet; ye also ought to wash one another's feet. For I have given you an example, that ye should do as I have done to you. Verily, verily, I say unto you, The servant is not greater than his lord; neither he that is sent greater than he that sent him. If ye know these things, happy are ye if ye do them." – John 13:3-17

The Master of all creation, the Lord of all, humbled Himself and washed the feet of His disciples. He did it intentionally to set an example of giving to others and then taught that the disciples would be blessed (happy) if they did the same.

By that very act, before the moment of His greatest sorrow, He sowed toward His future joy. Jesus demonstrated that the highest state of happiness was in doing a kind act or service for someone else.

What are we willing to do in order to be blessed later?

Take a moment to think about it. Instead of isolating ourselves from the world in our hurt, we should dive deep into it and help someone else. Go preach the gospel. Pray for the sick. Bless someone less fortunate. Bake a cake. Sing a song at a nursing home. Visit a homeless shelter. Start a non-profit organization. Make someone dinner. Go ahead. Bless someone and you too will be blessed.

"I have shewed you all things, how that so labouring ye ought to support the weak, and to remember the words of the Lord Jesus, how he said, It is more blessed to give than to receive." – Acts 20:35

Two Lives That Touched Nations

It was a somber and gray day in November 2003. I had returned from a funeral service for the father of one of our Freedom Worship Center church ministers at the time and was preparing to attend a prayer meeting that night with a Vietnamese congregation that I was overseeing on the east side of San Jose. Nothing seemed unusual, but as the sun set the events of that day would end up marking my life, my ministry, and the lives of many afterwards.

As we began the prayer service, a call came in that quickly spread within our small, tight-knit community of believers. Something terrible had happened – there was a major car accident on the 280 freeway near Palo Alto and five of my Freedom congregants were involved. Early details were sketchy and it took hours to actually piece together what had happened with various members calling me, and some driving to the scene of the accident to speak to those in authority. I asked the people at the prayer meeting to pray hard for those involved. When the accounts were confirmed, the final story was not what I wanted to hear.

A group of five church members leaving from the same funeral as I did earlier that day were involved in a major car crash. Only three of the five passengers in the Isuzu SUV that flipped on the freeway survived the accident. The two that did not walk away from the scene were my junior youth leader and one of my youth.

My heart sank within me as the calls from their mothers started to ring on my phone.

I prayed to God for the courage to inform them of their worst fears.

Hanh Do was the daughter of one of my members, a beautiful young lady and a bright shining star in our community and congregation for the two years that she attended. Loved by everyone, she had just graduated as the valedictorian of San Jose High School and had set her sights on greater achievements at the university level. Even more pleasant than her heart-warming smile was her passion for Jesus and love for people. At just nineteen, she was a strong, positive influence on the adolescents around her. I had asked her earlier that year to join our youth leadership team as a junior leader and began to mentor her for the ministry. She left for heaven that day just a month shy of her twentieth birthday.

Amber Bazan, on the other hand, stepped into our downtown community church when she was only 7 years old. I saw her grow up over the years whenever she was able to attend our services. A few years passed where she stopped coming altogether, and then one day, she was back – now as a teenager. However, this time things were different. She decided to give her life completely to Christ and was water baptized in the swimming pool of my apartment complex. As her pastor, I was thrilled to see that the little girl I called "mi hija" ("my daughter" in Spanish) had grown up to become a beautiful, caring, and godly young lady. Just two weeks after her baptism, she also entered Paradise with Hanh in that fatal car crash.

With their passing, the collective heart of our faith community was breaking and nothing on earth could mend it. The hardest thing I've ever had to do to was to tell both Hanh and Amber's mothers that their daughters were not coming home.

I've never heard such anguish come out of the human soul. Nor do I ever wish to experience it again. They screamed, fainted, cried, and prayed fervently and all I could do was cry with them and tell them that I was sorry while praying inwardly for God to help us all. They were inconsolable and we all broke down with them.

My faith was shaken. I wasn't sure if my congregations could recover from such a painful event. I wasn't sure if I could personally recover from it.

And yet, in the midst of all my doubts, fears, brokenness, and tears in the days following the incident, these thoughts would cross my mind, "If you give up, the loss of their lives will have been for nothing. Hanh gave her life to serve Christ and others. You taught her that. Amber recommitted herself to Christ. You influenced her in that decision. Let their lives mean something. Live in such a way that would honor them. Continue to help others like they would have, if they were still alive on earth."

In that moment, I knew what I had to do. I resolved to press onward carrying the memory of them in my heart.

As I tearfully shared the accomplishments of their young lives at both of their funerals, I made an inner vow to continue to honor God and serve people as a tribute to them for the rest of my life. At both funeral services, in their honor, I closed my eulogy messages by inviting their friends and family to invite Jesus into their hearts and lives. Hundreds of youth and family members responded by raising their hands and many wept openly as they prayed to receive Him at both services. I knew that my life and ministry would never be the same again.

At their funerals, Hanh and Amber touched more people for Christ than they ever did in their lifetimes. They ignited the fire that still drives me today to reach out and help others all over the world, and in the process of helping others, I realized that it also helped me to heal.

If I was the only one whose life had changed for the better because of these special young ladies, I would have been satisfied. Instead, others also became instruments of compassion, giving their lives over to good causes, and initiate inner healing from their loss.

One such person was Hanh's mother, Nina, who came to me about a year after her daughter's passing. She told me that she wanted to serve God in the nations as a missionary to Southeast Asia and asked for my blessing and support. She felt that she could do it now that her daughter was in heaven and her older children were independent and successful. I blessed her and encouraged her to follow Christ wherever He was leading her. Somehow, I knew that for her, the only way she would find true healing of the heart for her tragic loss was to reach out and serve others on the other side of the world, which she is still doing to this day.

Sometimes, the best path to initiate healing is to give ourselves away in the service of others. Both Nina and I found this to be true for our lives. Let's remember that Jesus said, "It *is* more blessed to give than to receive" (Acts 20:35) and go out and find somebody to love.

Here is a suggested prayer for the heart to love, serve and help others:

"Heavenly Father, I ask for a servant's heart. As you heal my wounded heart, please remake it like Yours - generous and with a desire to love, bless and help others. In doing so, may I sow and reap the seeds of my own future happiness in life. Thank You for showing me that my life is significant and needed as I serve others and that what I do in life really does make a difference. Use me to bring the healing and help that others need for Your glory, honor, and praise. In Jesus' name, amen."

CHAPTER 9

A Friend In Need Is A Friend Indeed

"A friend loveth at all times, and a brother is born for adversity."
-Proverbs 17:17

The Lone Ranger Syndrome

As you seek to be made whole from the heartache, it's always best to surround yourself with strong, loving, positive and faith-filled people. God created us to be social beings. No man is an island and no man isolated can thrive or heal without social interaction.

One of the first truths God revealed about mankind when He created man in the garden was this:

"And the LORD God said, It is not good that the man should be alone; I will make him an help meet for him." -Genesis 2:18

As a Pastor, I can't tell you how many times I've seen people enduring hardships by themselves over the years, and not because others didn't care, but because they didn't want other people around.

I've had hurting people tell me angrily to ask people to stop calling or visiting them. I wouldn't do it because it goes against what God's Word declares. It's not good for any man or woman to be alone, especially when they are hurting.

True friends will love at all times, good and bad, and a brother is born for the day of our adversity. This simply means that God has placed people in our lives for a reason and a season. They are there to help us in our time of pain and suffering, our time of need. Whatever happens, don't shut the people out who love you the most. Let them be there. Their presence will help you heal even if they have nothing to say. Learn not to be a Lone Ranger. Even he had Tonto faithfully by his side.

The Body Has Many Members

If you're a follower of Christ, then you are a part of His body and He is the head. Just like your own body, it has many parts. Each part makes up the whole organism. Together, we make up the complete body of Christ. The eye can't say to the ear that it doesn't need it. Neither can the hands say to the feet that they are not necessary any more. That would be ridiculous. Here's what they would say if those body parts were hurt:

Eyes: *"Ears! Are you there? Yes? Oh good! Because I can't see right now. I'm damaged and hurt pretty badly. I can't see too well. I really need you to hear for me so we don't get hit by a car crossing this street! You got it?"*

Feet: *"Hey Hands! Help! Feet here. We can't walk right now. We've been injured and need you to drag us to safety. Please do something!"*

When our natural bodies are injured, it goes into survival mode. That means every cell, organ, muscle, ligament, tendon, nerve, etc. starts to work together as a unit to save the whole body. Some parts even sacrifice themselves so that the whole body may live. As in the case of a deep cut, blood cells will actually sacrifice themselves to form a blood clot to stop the bleeding that could be life threatening. It's also true in the body of Christ. God has people around you who are willing to sacrifice their time and resources to show their love and care for you.

Start Your Own Support Group

"For by wise counsel thou shalt make thy war: and in multitude of counsellors there is safety." -Proverbs 24:6

"Ointment and perfume rejoice the heart: so doth the sweetness of a man's friend by hearty counsel." -Proverbs 27:9

Many times, going through a tragic situation opens doors for people to share about what they've been through. Don't be afraid to let them in. It will encourage you to know that there are others who have been where you are today. You're not the only person going through this. Chances are good that someone else has been down the same hard road.

The prophet Elijah found that out very quickly. He had just finished telling the Lord that he was the only prophet left in Israel who did not bow his knees to Baal. He believed it so much, he was starting to feel sorry for himself. God corrected him immediately by saying that he had preserved 7,000 other prophets who also did not bow their knees to the enemy! He learned a powerful lesson- that he was not alone in his trial. There will always be others who are walking or have walked the same path you are on.

Search for and get around those who will encourage you and give you the encouragement to persevere. Let people who have been there and overcome speak positive, uplifting words into your life. Let them advise you and heed their counsel. If they've already overcome the pitfalls of heartache, they can also teach you how to do the same.

Avoid Angry and Bitter People

Remember the principle from Chapter four, get better, not bitter? You need to be around people, but use wisdom who you allow into your inner circle during this sensitive time of pain and struggle. Being around those who've walked your path, but have not successfully healed or overcome may hinder your progress more than help. They will tell you how hard it is, what a drag it is to be you, and why you have nothing to look forward to. They will try to provide evidence of their claims by pointing to their own lives as an example of your potentially miserable future.

Don't believe the hype. Their lives are *their* lives. Your life is *your* life.

It's up to *you* what you make of your life.

You can't live their lives and neither can they predict yours. So don't let them be your prophets and make terrible predictions about your future. Trust God and those who have overcome their adversities and heartaches to guide you to safety.

Two are Better than One

I can't emphasize it enough. It's always easier to go through something with another person by your side. God is always there. It's also reassuring to know that *He has people prepared* who have the love and strength to uphold you when you don't.

"Two are better than one; because they have a good reward for their labour. For if they fall, the one will lift up his fellow: but woe to him that is alone when he falleth; for he hath not another to help him up." -Ecclesiastes 4:9-10

I remember that during my most difficult season, reeling from the effects of my broken engagement that my help came from the church youth group that I was helping to lead at the time. That group of precious young people helped me more than they'll ever realize. They looked to me as their source of spiritual inspiration, but I actually looked to them to provide me with companionship and the hope of a future in ministry. They helped me so much to know that I was needed after I was so heavily rejected by my ex-fiancée.

There is something powerful about finding that place where you are needed.

God set me up. He wanted to heal me by surrounding me with loving young people who appreciated me. They wanted me around. Their families wanted me around. Although I couldn't share with them the true difficulties I was facing emotionally, just being around them with their happy, energetic, and hopeful attitudes gave me the renewed hope that what I was going through was not going to last forever.

Right now, I believe there are people in your life who need you. Let them in, be there for them, and they will give you the courage to keep going another day.

I can imagine some readers thinking that they have no one who needs them. That's not true. There's probably a local homeless shelter filled with people that could use a friend or the nursing home on the other side of town. The local church could use some volunteers as well as the non-profit groups in your community. God has made a way for all of us to be needed by someone.

The worst thing to do is to *only* seek pleasure and escape from the pain of how you feel. Don't turn life off. There are wonderful people in that church, home group, or community center that can provide a warm, social environment for those that have few friends.

Divine Relationships

The Bible reveals that even the greatest heroes of faith needed friends in their times of adversity and brokenness.

David was a young man whose heart was broken when King Saul, whom he served, sought to kill him. He did have one true friend who helped him through all the years of hiding and that was the King's son, Jonathan. Every broken heart needs a Jonathan beside them.

The virgin Mary was supernaturally pregnant with the Son of God when she went to see her cousin Elizabeth who was also supernaturally pregnant with John the Baptist. This shared experience of carrying divine purpose helped them both support each other through their divine pregnancies as they fulfilled the plan of God.

Shadrach, Meshach and Abednego were friends in the Kingdom of Babylon who refused to bow down to the national idol. As a consequence, they were thrown together into a fiery furnace. As they faced the flames of death together as friends, God in His sovereignty intervened and allowed them to be untouched by the blazing fire that consumed everything except them.

The Apostle Paul had his support group of Barnabas, Silas, Luke, and Timothy among others in all his trials and persecutions. They supported him in his sufferings, imprisonments, shipwreck, stoning, and rejections throughout his missionary journeys.

Divine friendships have always been in the plans of God and He will also provide us with true friends who will share our pain and help us heal.

Friendship with Jesus

"A man that hath friends must shew himself friendly: and there is a friend that sticketh closer than a brother." -Proverbs 18:24

It's uplifting to know that when a man or woman chooses to follow Christ, the Scriptures promise a friendship with Him that is closer than any family member. In essence, it means that we will never be alone for the rest of our lives, even if no one befriends us. Jesus will never leave us nor forsake us even in our darkest hours and stand with us when our world is falling apart. He is a true and faithful friend and I found this to be true on my long, grueling road to healing.

For a year and a half, I was a broken man nursing my wounds. Each night, I would stare out my window into the dark night sky and gaze at the stars. I felt so alone and didn't know who I could talk to or call. Even if I did, I was sure most people wouldn't know what to say to me anyway. In one sense, I *was* inconsolable. It was then that my friendship with Jesus Christ truly began.

I spent all those lonely nights talking to Him. Sometimes crying before Him. When I felt restless at home, I would get in my car and drive for hours through the hills of San Jose just pouring my heart out to Him. Telling Him everything I was feeling– my frustrations, disappointments, disbelief at what happened, and that life just wasn't fair to me. I was angry, vulnerable, and honest with Him about everything. I envisioned him in my passenger seat carefully listening to every word that I shared and sometimes nodding in agreement.

Common activities that were meant for couples after my breakup felt extremely awkward to me. Simple things like going to the movies, the beach or dinner became frightening for an adjusting single man. I dreaded approaching the restaurant hostess and hearing them ask, "How many?" and sheepishly replying, "Oh, just one." But as I spent time with Him daily, I slowly learned to invite Him into all my personal affairs.

"Jesus, would you like to go to the beach today?"

"Let's have dinner tonight, Lord."

"Want to see a movie with me tonight, Jesus?"

My favorite expression became, "It's just You and me, Jesus."

Amazingly, with all of my invitations, He never once declined. I was drawing closer to Him daily and our friendship blossomed. He became not just the Savior of the whole world, but He became the Savior of my world – my *personal* Savior and my very best friend. A friend that sticks closer than any brother, even to this day.

Would you like to start a friendship with Jesus? Here is a suggested prayer for you:

"Heavenly Father, I don't want to be alone anymore. I need You in my life. Would You and Your Son, Jesus, be my friend? Draw me close to You and let our relationship grow. Thank You for calling me Your friend as I call You mine from this moment on and for all eternity. In Jesus' name, amen."

CHAPTER 10

Pursue An Attitude of Gratitude

"Gratitude unlocks the fullness of life. It turns what we have into enough, and more. It turns denial into acceptance, chaos to order, confusion to clarity. It can turn a meal into a feast, a house into a home, a stranger into a friend. Gratitude makes sense of our past, brings peace for today, and creates a vision for tomorrow."
-Melody Beattie

Heavenly Insight

It was a gray and cloudy day as I walked the floor of my bedroom crying out to God about being single. It had been a few years now since my breakup and I was slowly moving on with my life and finally healing inside. However, finding the "one" that I could share my life with hadn't happened yet. Because of this, I was angry and complaining to God. I knew it was wrong. I knew it wasn't helping my situation, but I kept going. Finally, when I had run out of things to grumble about, I heard his gentle voice lovingly correct me:

"Learn to be grateful for what you do have and stop looking at what you don't."

This profound statement by the Lord hit me like a hammer on the head and drove home a truth– I was looking at my situation from the wrong perspective. It dawned on me that day that in my state of singleness, I had the freedom to go where I wanted, when I wanted, with whoever I wanted. I had the freedom to serve God, work late, play basketball, etc. all without any time constraints and the responsibility of nurturing a relationship. I realized on that day that my future spouse and family would eventually come, but until they did, I had to count my blessings and learn how to enjoy the season of singleness that I was in.

"In positive psychology research, gratitude is strongly and consistently associated with greater happiness. Gratitude helps people feel more positive emotions, relish good experiences, improve their health, deal with adversity, and build strong relationships." - *Harvard Mental Health Letter Journal, November 2011*

As the saying goes, "It's not happy people that are thankful, it's thankful people that are happy" and now we have the psychological research to prove it. People who have made the decision to have an attitude of gratitude will eventually find happiness in their lives and deal with adversity better.

When I was willing to thank God for being single and for the seven years that I did have in my former relationship, then the real healing began. I began to thank God for all that I learned in those seven years – the good, the bad and the ugly. I vowed that the mistakes I made in that relationship I would not make again in the next one. I was willing to change the perspective of my situation into a positive one.

Half Empty or Half Full

I know we've all heard the analogy for life in the picture of the glass filled halfway with water. Some will see it and say that the glass is half empty and others will see the same glass and say that it's half full. The point of the metaphor is not what answer is right or wrong because the truth is that both answers are right. Life is what you make of it. How you look at a situation many times will determine the decisions that you make in it and eventually the outcome of it.

If the glass is half empty in your situation, it just means that whatever is left will soon be gone. If it's half full, it means that it's on its way to being filled to the top. One perspective is negative and one is positive. When we choose to be sincerely thankful, it is always a positive perspective. The truth is that *we should be thankful we even have a glass!*

It's difficult to hate someone when you're truly thankful for them. It's almost impossible to remain bitter when you're thankful for the time that you did have with that special someone. In my case, I was also thankful for the next phase of my life after that time was over– a season of singleness to serve God as hard as I could and prepare myself for my future spouse and family.

Be Thankful for Everything

"In every thing give thanks: for this is the will of God in Christ Jesus concerning you." -I Thessalonians 5:18

Again, we see the wisdom of God for us. He inspired the Apostle Paul to pen these immortal words almost 2,000 years ago from a cold, dark prison. Paul was not writing from a sunny beach and drinking coconut milk. It wasn't something he asked the followers of Christ to do and he himself was exempt from it. He wrote it and practiced it even in the toughest of circumstances because it is the will of God for every believer.

When the Lord adjusted my attitude that day, it was one of the most challenging things I had to change. I knew it was His will, but I had to ask for His help to do it. Eventually I learned to be thankful even for the things that didn't make sense to me or were painful. Through my newfound gratitude I began to have a positive outlook on life – that everything was somehow part of a bigger plan for my good. I had learned and am still learning at times how to bring the "sacrifice of praise, that is, the fruit of my lips *giving thanks* unto His name" (Hebrews 13:15).

God Looks for Worshipers

"But the hour cometh, and now is, when the true worshippers shall worship the Father in spirit and in truth: for the Father seeketh such to worship him." -John 4:23

Jesus taught the woman at the well that God seeks those who worship Him in spirit and truth. Intuitively, I always knew that the quickest way to get God's attention was to worship Him sincerely. Later, when I read this verse, His words of truth confirmed it. God seeks those who genuinely worship him. He is drawn toward and actively searching for those who will worship Him. Just think about it. As much as you are searching for God in your pain and heartache, when you begin to worship, He is also looking for you! When He shows up, your breakthrough has arrived.

Another example of this truth can be found in the story of the Apostle Paul and Silas when they were beaten and jailed in Philippi for casting a demon out of a young fortune teller (Acts 16:18-26). At midnight, with their feet in the stocks and their bodies bruised and in pain from the beatings that day, they began to pray and sing praises to God. Now that's an attitude of gratitude! When they did, the Scriptures record that the jail began to shake until everyone's chains broke and the prison doors opened. What happened in that jail? God showed up and set the captives free because His worshipers started praising Him.

What will God do when you begin to praise and worship Him?

Now you can find out. Take a moment and begin thanking Him.

Worship Lifts Heaviness

"To appoint unto them that mourn in Zion, to give unto them beauty for ashes, the oil of joy for mourning, the garment of praise for the spirit of heaviness; that they might be called trees of righteousness, the planting of the LORD, that He might be glorified." -Isaiah 61:3

According to this Scripture in the Book of Isaiah, there is beauty for our ashes. This is figurative language for hope in the darkest hours of our lives. The ashes represent death or the moments so painful that it feels like we are dying. In those moments, God promises that something beautiful will come out of it; that there is beauty for our ashes.

In this same verse, God also promises joy for our mourning. No explanation is needed here. He longs to bring a smile back to our grieving faces.

The third metaphor in that verse declares that the spirit of heaviness is lifted when it is replaced by a garment of praise. Praise is the "fruit of our lips giving thanks to His name" as mentioned previously. Of course, this is not a literal garment that we put on like a jacket or shirt, but an attitude of praise, thanksgiving and worship. We should be wearing an attitude of gratitude daily. When we do, the spirit of heaviness must leave, joy will replace mourning, and the beauty for our ashes is revealed.

Are you ready to make an attitude adjustment like I did? Here is a suggested prayer for you:

"Heavenly Father, please help me to see my painful circumstances in a new light. Grant me Your grace to be thankful at all times and in all situations. Help me to practice an attitude of sincere gratitude from this moment on and for the rest of my life. As I worship You, please grant me Your comforting presence and mighty delivering hand. I will trust You now for heaviness to lift, joy to return and beauty to be revealed in my ashes. In Jesus' name I thank You, amen."

CHAPTER 11

One Day at a Time

"A journey of a thousand miles begins with a single step"
- Laozi

The Long Road to Recovery

It was about six to eight months into my healing process when I had dinner with a friend. As we sat and conversed, I opened up and told him that it still hurt every single day. Even though my heartache was an emotional and psychological one, I literally felt *physical* pain in my chest constantly. It was there when I woke up each morning and when I laid myself down to sleep each night. He sat there and being a good friend, just listened, feeling as helpless as I did in my situation. In spite of how I felt, I continued to practice the Scriptural principles for healing that I had discovered. There were many times that I thought I would never be able to feel true peace again and move forward with my life.

Then one day I woke up and realized that it didn't hurt any more. I felt no pain. The ache in my heart was gone. I couldn't even pinpoint the exact moment that Jesus took it away. It just stopped hurting inside. I was finally free at last! I was so elated and thankful at the same time!

My whole journey toward healing took over a year and a half. Almost two years of my life was spent in recovery, but it was well worth it. I had come out on the other side. I had overcome heartache and become a wiser, stronger, and better man. I had learned to lean on Christ as my helper in my fiery trial and He had proven Himself mighty to deliver me from my prison of pain. It was a long, grueling trip, but it taught me the beauty of the faithfulness and perseverance of this loving God.

Let Patience Work

"But let patience have her perfect work, that ye may be perfect and entire, wanting nothing." – James 1:4

To be patient is defined in Merriam Webster's Dictionary as *the capacity to bear pain or trials calmly or without complaint and to be steadfast despite opposition, difficulty or adversity.* The Elder James in this verse advises us to "let" patience work. In other words, we need to allow (give permission to) the virtue of patience so that we can be made perfect or whole and lack nothing. According to his counsel, good things really do come to those wait.

We live in a very fast paced world today. We have fast food, microwave dinners, instant coffee, and on demand entertainment. As the quality of being fast becomes equated with the benefits of a good life, if we're not careful, the ability to be patient and wait for our complete recovery may seem outdated and foolish. However, nothing could be farther from the truth.

There are many things in life that still require a set amount of time to get the most benefit from it. Things like a home cooked meal made from scratch or the nine months it takes to conceive and deliver a child. Let's not forget that it requires time to truly get to know someone as well as work out the differences when two people don't see eye to eye. It still takes time for a tree to grow, a flower to bloom, a child to mature, and a heart to heal.

Biblical Examples of Epic Endurance

The Scriptures are filled with mighty men and women of faith who had the God-given ability to outlast their storms and thrive.

The Book of Job reveals that troubles come to everyone including the righteous, but it's the ability to endure that determines the final outcome. Job was a God-fearing man who lost everything in a short period of time – his marriage, his children, his possessions, and his health. The one thing he did not lose was his faith in God. Because of his patient endurance through his season of heartache, God restored and blessed him with twice as much as he had before the calamity came. He stands out in the Old Testament as a prime example of patience so much that James wrote to believers in his letter in the New Testament that everyone should imitate the "patience of Job" (James 5:11).

Abraham and Sarah are another great Scriptural example of a couple who waited patiently for God to fulfill His promise to them. The Book of Genesis records from chapters 12-21 that Abraham and his wife Sarah were a barren couple. He was seventy five years old when God appeared to him and promised him a son. It wasn't until he was one hundred years old that he finally saw Sarah give birth to his promised son, Isaac. He waited twenty five long years against all odds to become a father and eventually, a father of many nations. They were a power couple whose faith and patience eventually obtained the miraculous promise of God (Hebrews 6:12-15).

Moses waited forty years to be chosen by God as the deliverer of Israel after he left Egypt and then another forty years after wandering the wilderness to bring them the second time to the entrance of the promise land. That's an epic eighty years of waiting to fulfill his mission in life.

Let's not forget Moses' faithful leaders, Joshua and Caleb, who patiently waited forty long years with him in the wilderness to finally have their opportunity by God to lead the children of Israel into the promise land after his passing.

These just a few examples of patient endurance in the Bible, but the real question is… *how long are you willing to wait to receive your complete inner healing?*

You can Handle More Than You Think

"There hath no temptation taken you but such as is common to man: but God is faithful, who will not suffer you to be tempted above that ye are able; but will with the temptation also make a way to escape, that ye may be able to bear it." – I Corinthians 10:13

There will be days when you think you can't go on because of the pain you're experiencing. I've had plenty of those. Yet God remains faithful and will always make a way of escape if we don't quit. He knows our capacity and how much we can handle and will not give us more than we can bear.

What this means is that the heartache you're experiencing is actually something you were built to handle. When God created you in your mother's womb, He already foreknew you and gave you the ability to bear up under all the hurts and pains that you will eventually face in your life. You were actually born to overcome and you can handle much more than you think you can.

Never Ever Give Up

"And let us not be weary in well doing: for in due season we shall reap, if we faint not." – Galatians 6:9

Your healing breakthrough could be a moment away or a month away, but you'll never know the joy of being made whole if you quit. On the other hand, if you'll let patience operate, it will give you the ability to persevere until your healing manifests.

Learn to take things one day at a time, one step at a time, and eventually you'll realize that you've reached your destination. Trust the process. It's not magic. It's the law of the universe. The Word of Almighty God. You will eventually reap what you sow.

Here is a suggested prayer to let the patience of God operate powerfully in your life:

"Heavenly Father, I yield myself to the work of Your Holy Spirit in my life. I know that You have made a way of escape so that I can come out of my brokenness wiser, stronger, and better positioned for Your purposes for me. Help me to trust You and Your healing work in my heart. I will take life as a gift and live it one day at a time. Thank You for Your promise that I will eventually reap what I sow, and I am sowing into my recovery. In Jesus' name I pray, amen."

CHAPTER 12

Believe for a Happy Ending

*"He hath made every thing beautiful in his time: also he hath set
the world in their heart, so that no man can find out the work that
God maketh from the beginning to the end."*
– Ecclesiastes 3:11

God Writes the Last Chapter

Do you realize that at this very moment, God is working on your behalf? It may not seem like it to your five carnal senses (sight, smell, taste, touch, and hearing), but He is. God is Spirit and works in the unseen realms of the human spirit or heart. As you consistently apply the Scriptural principles that promise healing, you are giving God the freedom to make your heart whole again. While the end result is promised by our Creator, the time frame in which He does it is not. But one thing is very clear, everything will be made beautiful in *His* time.

From the Prison to the Palace

The promise of a beautiful ending reminds me of the story of Joseph in the book of Genesis. Joseph, the son of Israel, had been given two dreams by the Lord of his future calling as a great leader. However, when he shared his vision with his brothers they scoffed at him. Out of jealousy they eventually betrayed him and left him in a pit to die. He was picked up by a caravan of slave traders and sold as a slave in Egypt. We can be sure that he was truly heartbroken over the betrayal by his own brothers, but he sought to make the best of his plight. He patiently endured serving as a house slave until he was falsely accused of rape by the wife of his master, an Egyptian Captain of the Guard. He was sentenced to a life in prison. Things went from bad to worse. Just imagine how shattered his heart must have been. On the surface it seemed like his life was a series of never ending pain and heartache, but the Scriptures reveal that God was with him every step of the way. In a series of divine events and great favor from God, Joseph is finally brought from the prison to Pharaoh's palace where he became the governor of Egypt. What started as a dream in a seventeen year old boy grew into the destiny of a thirty year old man. In those thirteen years of pain, betrayal, heartache and perseverance, God was orchestrating a beautiful ending for his story. Joseph eventually reconciled with his brothers and in hindsight could clearly see the goodness of God in his life. He boldly told his brothers that what they had intended for evil in their act of betrayal, God turned it around for good by using it to fulfill his purposes and save many families in that region, including his own.

Double for All His Trouble

I mentioned Job in the last chapter in regards to his incredible patience, but an even more detailed look at his experience reveals not just an ancient story of loss, pain and heartbreak, but a wonderful outcome to the end of his life.

In the beginning of the book and throughout most of the story, God had been behind the scenes watching Job go through his heartache and pain caused by satan (with God's limited permission). But at the end of the book, God decides to visit Job for Himself and speak to him and his friends out of a whirlwind. God doesn't answer any of their questions about the sufferings of life or why mankind goes through heartache, but reminds them of His ultimate wisdom, power and goodness. As proof of His greatness, God gives Job what he didn't ask for – a full restoration of everything he lost. God restores his marriage, gives him more children, heals his body, extends his life, doubles his wealth and possessions, restores his reputation, and gives him back the respect of his friends. Job's ending was so much greater than his beginning! God gave him back *double* for all his trouble. The good news is that if he did it for Job, then I believe He is willing to do it for anyone who will put their trust in Him.

It really doesn't matter how we start, but it does matter to God how we end.

The Wounded Wanderer

If there was anyone who knew heartaches and sorrows in life and the goodness of God in spite of it all, it was King David. One of the most beloved characters in the Bible, he was the shepherd boy who walked onto a battlefield and slew a giant. Most people have heard of that part of David's amazing life story, but unless they've read the Scriptures, they don't know that his life *after* that major event was full of hurt, betrayal, rejection, trials, loss, loneliness, tragedy, and troubles. Hunted by his father-in-law, King Saul, and living in the wilderness as a wanderer, David longed for an end to his days as a fugitive. Even after King Saul died and he was crowned the King of Israel and Judah, his own son, Absalom, and trusted advisors tried to wrestle the united kingdom away from him. At the darkest period of his reign, he fell into scandal by killing a man for his wife, impregnating her, and then losing that child. Although he tried to keep his sins a secret, he was eventually exposed by God through the prophet Nathan.

David's life was a journey of heartache with some of it caused by the imposed will of others and some of it caused by his own foolish choices. It's for these same reasons that we love him because his story reflects how our lives often have the same internal and external conflicts along with their painful consequences. As the author of the majority of the Book of Psalms, his whole life journey can be summed up in his own prophetic words:

"Many are the afflictions of the righteous: but the LORD delivereth him out of them all." - Psalm 34:19

Through every hardship that David faced though, God was always a present source of help. He never left his side and stood faithfully to deliver him out of them all. Because of his acquaintance with suffering, David had the keen insight that the Lord is actually *near* to the afflicted and eventually *saves* them. David's life and heartfelt writings give us hope that God can take our tragedies and turn them into triumphs.

Things Can Work Together for Good

"And we know that all things work together for good to them that love God, to them who are the called according to his purpose."
– Romans 8:28

With God on our side, everything *can* work out for good. He knows the end from the beginning and if we'll trust Him, He will bring His plans to pass.

As you put your faith in Him and patiently chase your healing, I can't stress enough that you don't give up. The road may be long and hard, but the end will be in sight. God is faithful to His promises. He is at work in your heart even if you can't see it yet with your eyes.

I waited many years before sharing the truths in this book because I wanted to be sure that I experienced these principles firsthand. I have taken God at His Word and seen the results for myself. My story began with the painful breakup of a seven-year relationship, but it has now become my testament to a faithful, healing God. My test became my testimony. My mess became my message. My setback was only a setup for a great comeback. I have seen the goodness of the Lord in the land of the living.

As I stood waiting at the altar on that hot, gorgeous summer day in July 2003, my heart was overflowing with gratefulness. I was in a dreamlike state as my Pastor, Calvin Cook, asked the joyful gatherers to rise. The music began to play and all eyes turned toward the back of the garden terrace where we assembled. There, dressed in a beautiful white bridal gown and accompanied by her father stood the fulfillment of God's goodness to me. As she slowly proceeded to the front of the altar, tears began to form in my eyes as I recalled the painful moments of heartache from my previous relationship and the years of empty loneliness that ensued. I had chased the dream of recovering from my broken heart and God had fulfilled it. Now she stood before me, before God, before some of the very same family and friends who watched helplessly when my world was shattered years earlier by another woman. On that sunny day we were gathered for a different occasion. Not to mourn my loss like before, but to rejoice in what I had found. Not to grieve my brokenness, but to congratulate me for reaching the other side – finding wholeness and new love with the woman of my dreams.

"Whoso findeth a wife findeth a good thing, and obtaineth favour of the LORD." - Proverbs 18:22

Today, I'm grateful to be happily married to a beautiful and kind woman whom the Lord brought into my life years after my heartache and full recovery. I am also now the proud father of three beautiful children from this blessed union. God has done what He promised in His Word for me. He wrote the ending of my story. He worked everything out for my good and made everything beautiful in His time.

My Conclusion

The Lord walked with me through some of the most painful seasons of my life and at times had to carry me, but we reached the finish line of peace together. You will too, if you don't quit. Keep pushing forward one day at a time and you'll discover that Jesus *does heal* the brokenhearted.

If you've applied any of the Biblical principles mentioned in this book toward your life, I truly congratulate you for your courage.

I believe you are well on the road to *your* recovery.

As you're turning your heartache into hope, here is my suggested prayer for you to obtain your divine happy ending:

"Heavenly Father, I know that life is not a fairy tale and things don't always happen the way we want, but You can turn anything around for good. So that's what I ask for my life today. Turn this heartache, pain and loss into something good. Make the ending of my story beautiful in Your time. I ask for Your help to patiently move forward as I pursue my healing from brokenness. Give me the perseverance, strength, and determination to never give up until I reach that place of joy and wholeness again – a place where my heart no longer aches. May it be my heaven on earth. I thank You for Your great love and faithfulness toward me now and forever. In Jesus' name I pray, amen."

About the Author, Hoa Tong

Ministry

Hoa Tong began his walk with the Lord in the summer of 1987. Since then, he has served on the worship team, as an assistant Youth Pastor and finally as an Assistant Pastor for the Pentecostal Deliverance Church before becoming the co-founder and Senior Pastor of Freedom Worship Center, a multicultural inner-city church with an international outreach headquartered in San Jose, California.

Hoa launched Freedom in August 1997 with a handful of people and has grown Freedom's influence to include a thriving multicultural congregation, a weekly local television ministry reaching the San Francisco Bay Area, a volunteer run after school program to mentor kids on elementary school campuses within the city, and affiliate satellite churches and ministries internationally.

Locally, he spearheaded Freedom projects to help the poor and homeless. Projects such as "Elements - A night of fashion and fundraising" helped raise awareness and funding for Silicon Valley's social organizations and their causes. Charities such as The Salvation Army, City Team Ministries, Next Door Solutions to Domestic Violence, and Child Advocates have benefited from these projects. Hoa has also influenced Freedom members to serve the City of San Jose Government's Homeless Projects and each year oversees the Freedom Toy Giveaway Program to bless hundreds of needy families with gifts during the Christmas holiday.

Internationally, he has helped to plant and oversee satellite churches in the Philippines, Peru, Ecuador and Colombia. Hoa was also instrumental in partnering Freedom with Fields of Glory International based in Sacramento, CA to plant a Church on the outskirts of Lagos, Nigeria in Africa.

In addition to Freedom, Hoa also presides over the Vietnamese Grace Community Church in San Jose, CA and sits on the Board of Advisors for X-Factor Ministries in Santa Clara, CA and Breaking Free Revival Center in Fresno, CA.

World Missions

Hoa has traveled the globe as a missionary since 1996. In the nations, he serves the people, the local church, and government with humanitarian efforts in facilitating donations of food, fresh water, clothing, medicine and personal hygiene products as well as sharing the life changing message of the gospel. He has led countless thousands to the saving knowledge of Jesus Christ on television, radio and in-person ministry events worldwide.

Hoa has also ministered and served in the following nations: Philippines, Vietnam, Indonesia, Singapore, India, New Zealand, Ecuador, Peru, Colombia, Brazil, Spain, England, Burundi and Nigeria.

Leadership

A strong believer in Kingdom leadership principles, Hoa has influenced and released leaders to serve in communities both locally and globally. He has spoken at leadership seminars in the Philippines, Peru, and Vietnam for both churches and universities. Hoa has also taught leadership principles at the Silicon Valley Ministerial Institute and annually at Freedom Worship Center to raise more leaders from within the organization.

Professional

Hoa is an award-winning creative director with over 18 years of experience on both the agency and corporate side in the marketing, design, advertising, and digital signage industry. He has managed, as well as, developed creative departments from the ground up. His creative work has enabled top tier and start up clients to succeed in both online and offline traditional media, lead generation, demand creation, new media, social media, and experiential design.

In the span of his career, he's developed creative for some of the world's top Fortune brands - Cisco, Disney, ExxonMobil, Kodak, Hitachi, Nero, Philips, Intel/McAfee, Microsoft/Skype, Shell, The San Francisco Giants, TSMC, and Marvell among others. His creative work over the years has won American Advertising Federation (ADDY) awards, Davey Awards, and a Business Marketing Association Award. In summary, Hoa demands creative that demands attention.

Hoa is honored to be an alumnus of San Jose State University, graduating with honors.

International Awards and Offices

Hoa has been awarded with an honorary doctorate degree (Ph.D) in Philosophy in Humanities from Kayiwa International University in Uganda, Africa. He is also a recipient of the esteemed Golden Rule International Award and conferred as an honorary Goodwill Ambassador of Peace by the Interfaith Peace Building Initiative based in Ethiopia. Hoa also serves as an Advisor for the Ambassador at Large of Burundi, Africa – Dr. Clyde Rivers.

Personal

Hoa is happily married to his beautiful wife, Leslie, and is the proud father of three wonderfully blessed children– Zoe, Lukas, and Judah.

About Freedom Worship Center

Freedom Worship Center began as a little house church by a few immigrant families from the Philippines in the 1960's. That founding Filipino congregation thrived until the early 1990's. By August 1997, God had called the church to re-launch as Freedom Worship Center, a multicultural, non-denominational church to meet the needs of blended families in the Silicon Valley and internationally.

Today, Freedom Worship Center remains an intimate faith community, but has grown in influence to include a local television ministry reaching the San Francisco Bay Area, after school programs to mentor children in San Jose, yearly missions trips to preach the gospel and perform humanitarian work around the world, and plant satellite churches and establish affiliate ministries in the Philippines, Peru, Ecuador, Colombia, and Vietnam. Freedom is also involved in local community work and the spreading of the God's love through the urban arts such as musical theater, art shows, concerts, film, and benefit fashion shows.

Senior Pastor Hoa Tong and the ministry staff invite you to visit Freedom anytime you are in the San Jose / San Francisco Bay Area. You'll be loved, supported, and encouraged to fulfill your destiny in Christ and influence nations for the glory of God and His Kingdom.

For more information, please contact us at:

www.freedomwc.org
www.facebook.com/freedomworshipcenter
email: freedomwc@aol.com
phone: (408) 297-8508

Made in United States
Troutdale, OR
08/23/2023

12326826R00058